The Integrated Enterprise
Excellence System

Advance Praise for
The Integrated Enterprise Excellence System

"IEE represents the best of best practices in measurement and improvement. It transcends Lean Six Sigma and the Balanced Scorecard. It's a powerful business system that blends analytics with innovation and arms everyone in the organization with the tools needed to contribute to success. Aptly named, it truly integrates enterprise excellence."
—Mike Jones, Past President, ASQ

"Forrest's Integrated Enterprise Excellence (IEE) system is not simply a methodology for doing Six Sigma projects. IEE offers an overall management system that provides the framework where companies can implement and benefit from Dr. Deming's methodologies."
—Bill Wiggenhorn, Retired President of Motorola University, currently Vice Chairman of GEM Global Edu-tech Management Group

"Challenging the status quo of traditional metrics and performance indices, the IEE approach will resonate with CEO's, while also relating to those on the production floor."
—Jesse Hamilton, Director of Process Excellence, Daltile

"Very well written, informative, clear and accessible."
—Bob Ashenbrenner, Senior Computer Architect, Motion Computing
Previously Director of Engineering for Dell's Notebook PCs

"[Forrest] takes us to the next level of skill development using Six Sigma to improve customer service and bottom line growth."
—Janet L Hammill, Business Process Excellence Lead, MBB, Rohm and Haas Company

"This is a wonderful and insightful reference book."
—René Kapik, Medical Team Leader, Precision Fabrics Group

The Integrated Enterprise Excellence System:
An Enhanced, Unified Approach to Balanced Scorecards, Strategic Planning, and Business Improvement

Forrest W. Breyfogle III
Founder and CEO
Smarter Solutions, Inc.

Forrest@SmarterSolutions.com
www.SmarterSolutions.com
Austin, Texas

BridgewayBooks

The Integrated Enterprise Excellence System: An Enhanced, Unified Approach to Balanced Scorecards, Strategic Planning, and Business Improvement

Published by Bridgeway Books in cooperation with Citius Publishing, Inc, Austin, TX

For more information about our books, please write to us, call 512.478.2028, or visit our website at www.bridgewaybooks.net.

Library of Congress Control Number: 2007936770

ISBN-13: 978-1-934454-11-4
ISBN-10: 1-934454-11-7

Cover concept design by Priyanka Kodikal.

10 9 8 7 6 5 4 3 2 1

To my beloved wife, Becki, who has made so many sacrifices in support of my work.

Contents

Foreword

What an exciting and challenging time to be in business! The world is shrinking, customers are more demanding, margins are being squeezed, technologies are on a fast track, and international competition is relentless. This demands the best in all of us!

Managing an enterprise with these conditions could be a recipe for disaster unless you have a plan, framework and a clear path forward. With the challenges of creating, sustaining and surviving, organizations must have a more comprehensive yet versatile management system – one which goes beyond traditional quality, measurement and control systems.

Forrest Breyfogle's state-of-the-art Integrated Enterprise Excellence (IEE) system firmly establishes a new capability for an organization to fully control, predict and react innovatively to demands with refreshed goals. Under IEE, the organization is achieving what Breyfogle calls the 3 Rs of business: everyone is doing the right things right at the right time.

Primacy has not only improved the quality of everything we do after adopting IEE's methods, but equally vital it has increased Primacy's marketplace position and our overall performance. Six Sigma projects are fine if they support our corporate goals, but they tend to work in isolation. IEE helps a worldwide service company like ours to identify and maintain the continuity and growth of our overall business focus.

Smarter Solutions, Inc. has perfected a management process that has been developed by using decades of modern enterprise management theory and practice to establish a process for both operational and corporate levels in creating new insights and techniques to sustain, innovate and grow a business under the most demanding conditions.

Organizations become data driven with IEE instead of what seems to be conventional wisdom by blending analytics with innovation to make decisions. Accounting irregularities are a thing of the past and management at all levels understand that setting goals without a roadmap does not improve processes.

Decision making within IEE's structure is guided by a disciplined look at high level metrics that are not bounded by calendar year or quarterly measurements. Another invaluable element of its roadmap is in understanding that some traditional measurements can motivate wrong activities.

IEE's organizational structure measures only what matters and every metric has an owner. An organization's priorities are determined by an Enterprise DMAIC (Define, Measure, Analyze, Improve, Control) process that extends up and down the value chain.

Gone are the days when projects are selected in isolation from each other. Improvements are made at the periphery of an organization instead of in critical success paths – where there are low hanging fruit projects, but improvement efforts stall soon after.

Innovation is integrated with analytics by IEE's process in a balance appropriate for an organization's particular culture and strategy. The project execution roadmap truly integrates Lean and Six Sigma activities. This is true regardless of whether the environment is manufacturing or transactional. All other process improvement tools are fully integrated.

All work is standardized to reduce variability and improve quality. There is zero-level ambiguity regarding internal and customer requirements. Material and information flows are seamless.

With measurements in place at both operational and corporate levels, there is zero potential for improper movement of resources from one entity to another. There is no employee avoidance of responsibility or use of metrics to hide productivity shortfalls rather than monitor them. In other words, it prevents problems like those at Enron, Dell and other companies.

In contrast with what many businesses experience, gains from an IEE structure are perpetual. The system stays in place whether or not there is management continuity, changes in the competitive environment or the economy.

Forrest Breyfogle has now firmly established a well-deserved reputation as an innovative developer of enhanced management systems capable of linking the attainment of business goals to a set of well documented management tools.

The development of Integrated Enterprise Excellence is a new level of excellence in an increasingly challenging business environment through the integration of successful techniques in a wide range of management disciplines.

This book is rich in content with examples of how specific analytical and decision support techniques can be merged to create a climate for perpetual enterprise growth and progress.

IEE truly leads the options for management at all levels by embedding in its processes established methods like Lean, Six Sigma and Design of Experiments. Traditional measurements and controls are challenged by documenting alternative methods, using real world examples, to eliminate hazards. Innovative thinking is encouraged and provides a clear path for successful enterprises of any size.

IEE's philosophy creates leaders that are teachers and teachers that are leaders.

Matt Spinolo
President and CEO
Primacy Relocation

Preface

The Integrated Enterprise Excellence (IEE) system introduced in this book is a set of management techniques that when implemented effectively can achieve maximum, measurable, predictable, and sustainable bottom line results for an organization.

This book provides solutions and insight to managers and leaders for the following:

- Scorecard metrics are leading to wrong and perhaps organizationally destructive behaviors.
- Systems for goal setting and tracking to these targets are not benefiting the company as a whole.
- Corporate strategies and directives are often not data-determined and can lead to metrics and activities that are not necessarily benefiting the whole organization.
- Executive governance systems can lead to activities that are jeopardizing the company's long-term health in order to meet short-term goals.
- Efforts to improve corporate growth and revenue are not targeting the areas that could deliver the most gains.
- Process improvement efforts are silo organizational activities, which do not impact the business bottom line as a whole.
- Problem firefighting does not focus on root cause analysis and the achievement of sustainable corrective actions.
- Innovative ideas that can truly benefit the business as a whole are not occurring, not what the customer truly wants/needs, or not transitioned to the marketplace in a timely fashion.
- Systems for orchestrating employee day-to-day activities are not focused on what should be done to maximize benefits for the overall system.

OVERVIEW

In his book, *Good to Great*, Jim Collins (2001) describes a level five leader as someone who is not only great when he is leading an organization but also as one who enables the organization to remain great after leaving it. I describe the level-five-leader-created legacy as being a *Level Five System*. This book illustrates how IEE can be used to formulate a Level Five System.

The book highlights common business systems issues and presents IEE as an enhanced methodology that can improve organizational efficiency and effectiveness. It documents a set of best practices derived from the strengths of past systems – illustrating the basics of structuring IEE metrics and a no-nonsense roadmap to initiate process improvement and achieve substantial benefits. It takes Lean Six Sigma and the balanced scorecard to the next level in the pursuit of excellence in the enterprise.

Most readers will be able to relate many of the described issues and examples. Some will find this book to be a stimulus for organizational change. The 3-volume series, *Achieving Enterprise Excellence: Beyond Lean Six Sigma and the Balanced Scorecard*, provides the how-tos{AQ} of IEE implementation, as described in the Appendix.

NOMENCLATURE AND SERVICE MARKS

The glossary and list of acronyms and symbols at the back of this book are a useful reference for understanding unfamiliar statistical terms, acronyms and symbols. Book and publication references are also located near the back of this book and will be referenced using the syntax (Author Name, Publication Date).

Integrated Enterprise Excellence, IEE, Satellite-level, 30,000-foot-level, and 50-foot-level are registered service marks of Smarter Solutions, Inc. In implementing the programs or methods identified in this text, you are authorized to refer to these marks in a manner that is consistent with the standards set forth herein by Smarter Solutions, Inc., but any and all use of the marks shall inure to the sole benefit of Smarter Solutions, Inc. Business way of Life and Smarter Solutions are registered service marks of Smarter Solutions, Inc.

ACKNOWLEDGMENTS

I want to thank those who have helped with the creation of this volume. Lynn Cheshire helped through her editing and layout improvement suggestions. Rick Haynes provided many great suggestions and inputs to this volume. Bob Ashenbrenner, John Hannon, Joe Knecht, Cheryl Ray, and John Watson gave great detailed and very helpful manuscript feedback. Fred Bothwell provided great manuscript and marketing inputs, along with superb publishing and printing coordination.

Thanks also need to go to those who gave other helpful improvement suggestions or helped in some other way in the overall process: Bill Baker, David Behrendsen, Dan Egger-Belandria, Becki Breyfogle, Wes Breyfogle, Alvin Brown, Bob Cheshire, Sonja Cline, Larry Dalton, Donn Fisher, Joe Flagherty, Kiran Gurumurthy, Jesse Hamilton, Bob Jones, Arch Holder, Lally Marwah, Todd Minnick, George Nicholas, Mallary Musgrove, Andy Paquest, Tanya Roberts, Janet Shade, Frank Shines, Jeannine Siviy, Gary Wietharn, Brian Winterowd, Johnny Yu, and Brian Zicvis.

Statistical analyses were conducted using Minitab. Flowcharts were created using Igrafx.

ABOUT SMARTER SOLUTIONS, INC., CONTACTING THE AUTHOR

Your comments and improvement suggestions for this book-volume series are greatly appreciated. For more information about business measurements and improvement strategies, sign up for our newsletter or e-mail us for a free initial business consultation.

FORREST W. BREYFOGLE III
Smarter Solutions, Inc.
11044 Research Blvd., Suite B-400
Austin, Texas 78759 USA
Forrest@SmarterSolutions.com
512-918-0280
www.SmarterSolutions.com

1

Challenges Facing Leaders – An Integrated Enterprise Excellence Resolution

These are difficult times for organizational leaders. There are the demands of the supply chain, board members, investors, regulators, and employees, often with conflicting priorities. The expectation of quarterly improvements must be balanced by the necessity for meeting long-term needs. Foreign competition and domestic labor costs erode margins. An innovation by a competitor can create havoc. Unimagined varieties of unforeseen events can divert leadership from its true role and put it in firefighting mode.

The complexity of business is growing exponentially as data becomes more readily available, creating still more challenges. Senior management can feel a lack of control – vulnerable to being manipulated, unaware of the improper and even illegal movement of resources from one entity to another. Employees can be avoiding responsibility, playing the blame game, and using metrics to hide productivity shortfalls rather than monitor them. Without the proper enterprise management system these common issues will be uncontrollable.

Providing some relief programs such as Lean Six Sigma have helped many businesses make performance improvements. Usually, the results of the first few implementations are impressive because the goals were easily achievable, but the system is difficult to sustain. Though management may be satisfied with project execution, there is a nagging doubt about whether enterprise issues are being addressed. Quite often Lean Six Sigma projects as well as strategy statements show no direct alignment or specific direction in achieving corporate financial goals.

Many senior executives admit that there are significant gaps between what they should know about operations and what they do know. They cannot determine with certainty whether there are inherent flaws in critical operational processes. When asked to describe the progress their business is making, many will recite metrics but are not certain how they got to that point or if they can repeat the behavior. They may offer a snapshot of the company's status, while the real need is a continuous picture describing key outputs over time, along with the key inputs that contributed to the success/failure of the organization. In too many organizations, accurate forecasting has become a guessing game.

Management needs a measurement and improvement system that makes possible the orchestration of day-to-day activities so there is true business-needs alignment – a system that not only monitors operations for management, but also provides the entire workforce with information that can be used down the line to make sure everyone's performance directly supports corporate strategies or else becomes the target for corrective action. For any business to succeed, it must follow the three Rs of business: Everyone is doing the Right things and doing them Right at the Right time. Management's ultimate goal continues to provide maximum, measurable, predictable, and sustainable bottom-line results for the entire, integrated enterprise. Emergence of the process called Integrated Enterprise Excellence (IEE) makes all of these possible.

IEE is the result of a quarter century of work in the development and integration of a base set of statistical and non-statistical tools and their integration with each other. Keith Moe, retired Group Vice President of 3M's Electro and Communications Markets Group Division, considers IEE the most complete and effective operational management system available. He defines it as a process that allows management to accurately predict financial results, meet growth goals, maximize cash flow, force innovation, develop responsive supply chain dynamics, meet customer needs, improve employee performance, and avoid surprises.

IEE is a system of selected checks and balances that will stay in place regardless of management continuity, changes in competitive conditions, or the economic climate. As such, the methodology takes Lean Six Sigma and the balanced scorecard to a new level. It does not simply identify the flaws in an operational process; it determines whether the process itself is flawed. It does not replicate projects; it designs and replicates systems. It replaces firefighting with fire preventive actions.

It prevents the organization from executing projects that may be counterproductive. It helps organizations plan for the unplanable and combat efforts to use metrics in fraudulent ways. The methodology provides a no-nonsense performance measurement scorecard that serves as an enterprise-wide beacon for orchestrating improvement and innovative efforts so that profitability increases.

The IEE methodology is consistent with many of the quality principles of Dr. W. Edwards Deming and uses, at the enterprise level, the familiar Six Sigma define–measure–analyze–improve–control (DMAIC) roadmap.

This book presents a process for implementing Integrated Enterprise Excellence.

2

Business Systems Can Stimulate the Wrong Behavior

It is said that what we measure is what we get. However, we need to be careful of what we ask for. Some questions for thought:

1. Do your metrics promote the right kind of behavior?
2. Do your presentation and the reward plan that surrounds your metrics lead to the right kind of behavior?

First, we obviously would like to create metrics that lead to the right kind of behavior. To illustrate this, consider a call center's duration-of-hold-time metric. This metric makes good sense relative to assessing customer satisfaction; that is, long hold times would probably correlate to customer dissatisfaction. However, in isolation, this metric can drive the wrong behaviors unless safeguards are implemented to prevent abuse.

To illustrate this point, consider the focus that operators will give to achieve the targeted metric objective during understaffed peak call periods. Operators might simply answer the phone within the allotted time period, ask, "Can you hold, please?" and then quickly place the caller on hold for a much longer period.

It is not bad that the operator answered the phone and responded, asking that the caller to wait longer; however, this type of action should not be simply the result of wanting to make the overall duration-of-hold-time metric look good. Relative to recording the actual hold time for future customer satisfaction analyses, it would be better to capture the total hold time from initial connection until the incoming caller is connected to the appropriate person.

Second, we need data presentation and assessment formats that lead to the right kind of behavior, with appropriate reward systems in place to encourage this behavior. If an organization is measured solely on the meeting of goals, which might be arbitrary, bad things can occur. For example, Krispy Kreme shipped doughnuts that executives knew would be returned so that they would meet quarterly targeted objectives (Lloyd, 2005). Additionally Enron and, more recently, Dell made some decisions that enabled them to meet quarterly objectives but were poor in the long run. According to press reports, the senior management of Dell regularly falsified quarterly returns from 2003 through 2006 to create the appearance that the company had met sales goals (Richtel, 2007).

In my opinion, data presentation and interpretation are not given adequate consideration. This chapter discusses some traditional presentation formats. We will then examine these formats collectively, and I will offer an alternative reporting format that can lead to significantly improved actions from these metrics.

2.1   Performance Metrics and the Numbers Game

The book *Lean Thinking* (Womack and Jones, 1996) describes companies that have successfully implemented the Toyota Production System. Two companies featured in this book were Wiremold Company and Lantech, Inc. Two executives from these companies, Jean Cunningham and Orest Fiume, later wrote *Real Numbers: Management Accounting in a Lean Organization* (Cunningham and Fiume, 2003).

When *Real Numbers* was published, Jean Cunningham was the chief financial officer and vice president of Company Services for Lantech, Inc., and was a leader in the company's transformation to Lean. Orest Fiume had retired as vice president of Finance and Administration and director of Wiremold Company.

These financial executives from two highly regarded companies make many insightful statements regarding existing accounting departments and systems. I highly recommend this book and periodically will reference statements from it. Readers need to keep in mind that these statements are from financial executives in their fields of expertise.

Cunningham and Fiume (2003) make the following points:

- Information must... be easily understood and actionable. Over the years, however, managers have been forced to understand their own departments, not in terms of income and cost, but as variances and percentages that bear little relationship to reality (i.e. where variances mean the differences between what is expected and what actually occurs).
- Those same managers learned that variances could be nudged up or down to present a better picture of the operation – for instance, by using labor hours to make a million pieces of plastic that were not actually needed, even if that meant damaging the real business interests.
- Complex accounting created a kind of funhouse mirror, where a skinny man could look fat by simply shifting his position.

It is not uncommon for newspaper articles to make statements similar to the following (Petruno, 2006):

There is a sinking feeling among technology stock investors this summer – a feeling of history repeating.

At the start of 2002, the bear market of that era had been raging for nearly two years. Then came a wave of corporate scandals that showed the Enron Corp. debacle of late 2001 was no one-of affair.

As shares of Tyco International Ltd., Adelphia Communications Corp. and WorldCom Inc. collapsed in the first half of 2002 amid allegations of massive financial fraud by executives, demoralized investors began wondering whether they could trust any number on balance sheets and income statements.

The scandals helped fuel a last burst of panicked selling, driving down the Standard & Poor's 500 index nearly 30 percent in the first nine months of 2002 and the Nasdaq composite index by 40 percent.

Now, investors' faith in corporate accounting again is under siege. Over the past few months more than 65 companies, most of them technology companies, have disclosed that they were under scrutiny or investigation by federal authorities for possibly manipulating executives' stock option grants to boost the potential payoffs.

In another article, "CEO firings at a record pace so far this year" (Kelly, 2006), it is stated that "chiefs are being pushed out the door as directors abandon their laissez-faire approach to governance following the prosecutions at Enron Corp., World-Com, Inc., and other companies."

These high-profile illustrations highlight only the tip of the iceberg relative to how organizational metric reporting can lead to the wrong behaviors. Organizations need a leadership system to overcome a "laissez-faire approach to governance." I will later describe how the no-nonsense IEE approach addresses these issues.

The next section will describe the characteristics of a good metric. Sections 3.3, 3.6, and 3.7 will then illustrate how commonly used organizational internal functional metric tracking and reporting can stimulate the wrong behavior throughout the organization.

2.2   Characteristics of a Good Metric

We have all heard the clichés:

- You get what you measure.
- What you measure is what you get.
- If you don't measure it, you can't manage it.
- Tell me how I'm going to be measured and I'll tell you how I'll perform.
- You cannot improve what you can't measure.
- Garbage in, garbage out.
- If you don't measure it, it's just a hobby.

These clichés are true! Measurements need to be the processes' eyes, which stimulate the most appropriate behavior. Measurements need to provide an unbiased process performance assessment. When process output performance is not accurately seen and reported relative to a desired result, there is not much hope for making improvements. Generic measures for any process are quality, cost, and delivery. Most processes need a balance measurement set to prevent optimizing one metric at the expense of overall process health. Metrics can also drive the wrong behavior if conducted in isolation from the overall enterprise needs. When appropriate, the addition of a people measure assures balance between task and people management.

As an illustration, consider the last customer satisfaction survey form that you received. Do you think that a summary of responses from this survey truly provides an accurate assessment of what you experienced in your purchase process? My guess is that your response is no. It seems that often surveys are conducted so that the responses will be satisfactory but don't truly provide insight into what actually happens in a process.

Writing an effective survey and then evaluating the responses is not easy. What we would like to receive from a survey is an honest picture of what is currently happening in the process, along with providing improvement direction. A comment section in a hotel guest survey might provide insight to a specific actionable issue or improvement possibility.

> COMMON CAUSE: natural or random variation that is inherent in a process or its inputs.

Good metrics provide decision-making insight that leads into the most appropriate conclusion and action or nonaction. The objective is the creation of an entity that is measurable, auditable, sustainable, and consistent. Effective and reliable metrics require the following characteristics:

- *Business alignment*: Metrics consume resources for both data collection and analyses. Metrics need to provide insight to business performance, its issues, and its needs. Metrics surrounding your business alignment can be found by looking at your value chain.
- *Honest assessment*: Creating metrics so that the performance of someone or an organization will appear good has no value and can be detrimental to the organization. Metrics need to be able to provide an honest assessment, whether good, bad, or ugly.
- *Consistency*: Identified components in any metric need to be defined at the outset and remain constant. Criteria and calculations need to be consistent with respect to time.
- *Repeatability and reproducibility*: Measurements should have little or no subjectivity. We would like for a recorded measurement response to have little or no dependence on who and when someone recorded the response.

> SPECIAL CAUSE: Variation in a process from a cause that is not an inherent part of the current process or its inputs.

- *Actionability*: Often measures are created for the sake of measuring, without any thought as to what would be done if the metric were lower or higher. Include only those metrics that you will act on; that is, either remove a degradation problem or hold the gain. When the metrics response is unsatisfactory, organizations need to be prepared to conduct root-cause analysis and corrective or preventive actions.
- *Time-series tracking*: Metrics should be captured in time-series format, not as a snapshot of a point-in-time activity. Time-series-tracking can describe trends and separate special-cause from common-cause variability in predictable processes.

PREDICTABLE PROCESS: A stable, controlled process where variation in outputs is only caused by natural or random variation in the inputs or in the process itself.

- *Predictability*: A predictability statement should be made when time-series tracking indicates that a process is predictable.
- *Peer comparability*: In addition to internal performance measurements, benefits are achieved when comparisons can be made between peer groups in another business or company. A good peer comparison provides additional analysis opportunities, which can identify improvement possibilities.

Metric utilization requires commitment and resource allotments; hence, it is important to do it right. When organizations strive to become more metric driven, it is important to avoid metric-design and metric-usage errors. Common mistakes include the following:

- Creating metrics for the sake of metrics. Lloyd S. Nelson, director of Statistical Methods for the Nashua Corporation, stated, "the most important figures needed for management of any organization are unknown or unknowable" (Deming, 1986).
- Formulating too many metrics, resulting in no actions.
- Lacking metric follow-up.
- Describing metrics that do not result in the intended action.
- Creating metrics that can have subjective manipulation.

If not exercised effectively, metrics can become a dark force where good energy is absorbed by bad stuff – a black hole where good resources are lost.

2.3 Traditional Scorecards/Dashboards and Performance Metrics Reporting

A scorecard helps manage an organization's performance through the optimization and alignment of organizational units, business processes, and individuals. A scorecard can also provide goals and targets, helping individuals understand their organizational contribution. Scorecards can span the operational, tactical, and strategic business aspects and decisions of any business. A dashboard displays information so that an enterprise can be run effectively. A dashboard organizes and presents information in a format that is easy to read and interpret.

A performance metric is a performance-related measurement of activity or resource utilization. Year-to-date metric statements are one form of performance metric reporting, while other formats involve tables or charts.

> Performance-measure report-out formats can have a dramatic influence on behaviors. Many situations can have numerous report-out options.

Performance-measure report-out formats can have a dramatic influence on behaviors. Many situations can have numerous report-out options. Much unproductive work can be generated if the best scorecard/dashboard metric is not chosen.

This section describes some frequently used performance metrics and scorecard/dashboard reporting formats, which can create detrimental organizational behavior. Later sections of this chapter will introduce an alternative IEE scorecard/dashboard performance measurement system that allows organizational enterprise management systems to react more quickly to favorable or unfavorable circumstances.

Table 2.1 exemplifies one commonly used performance measure report out. This report format has calendar boundaries that reflect only quarterly and annual results. This type of chart does not present response data as though it were a result of internal processes that inherently have variability. In addition, this chart cannot identify trends, detect unusual events in a timely fashion, or provide a prediction statement.

Is there a consistent message presented in Table 2.1? Invariably you will get stories that cannot be verified in the chart.

Look at the third line. You might hear something like "We staffed up in 2002 to prepare for annexations, but they did not happen as quickly as expected. This drove our cost per call up. As we annexed in 2003, you can see it coming down. We are on track."

It may be a true story, but is it the whole cause as it is represented? It is a good bet that the presenter will describe many of the ups and downs in the table in a story format, where in reality much of this motion is the result of common-cause variability. Have you seen tables like this before?

This form of performance reporting and of other year-to-date metric statements typically leads to *stories*. This means that someone presenting this scorecard/dashboard will typically give an explanation for the up-and-down movements of the previous quarter or year. This is not dissimilar to a nightly stock market report of the previous day's activity, where the television or radio reporter gives a specific reason for even small market movements. This form of reporting provides little, if any, value when it comes to making business decisions.

> This form of performance reporting and of other year-to-date metric statements typically leads to stories.

Table 2.1: Traditional performance measures: tabular reporting (Austin, 2004).

Performance Measure	FY 2001 Actual	FY 2002 Actual	FY 2003 Actual	FY 2003 Amended	FY 2004 Amended
Percentage of customers satisfied with dispatch staff	99.99%	100%	99.99%	98%	98%
Percentage of priority one calls dispatched to field crews within 80 minutes of receipt	99.99%	99%	99.99%	95%	95%
Labor cost per customer call taken in Dispatch Operations	$4.20	$5.31	$5.09	$4.88	$5.09
Number of calls taken through Dispatch Operations	62,054	59,828	63,046	60,000	60,000
Number of priority one calls dispatched to field crews	5,797	4,828	6,686	5,000	6,500
Number of work orders and component parts (segments) created in database	8,226	4,724	7,742	5,500	6,700

Whether in a business performance measure or a stock market report, these reported causal events may or may not have affected the output. The individual measurement value may cause an alarm that triggers some corrective action, or the numbers may be viewed only as a simple report. In either case, most measurement variability is typically the result of the system's common-cause variations.

An alternative to table presentations for a data-driven company is chart presentations. For example, user guidelines from Quick-Base 2006 state, "What information do you want to show? This is always the first question you must ask yourself when creating a chart. For example, if you want to show what percentage each salesperson contributes to the bottom line, try a pie chart, which is great for showing how parts relate to a whole. Or maybe you'd prefer to show how each salesperson has been doing over the course of the year. In that case, a line chart might work best. That way you could plot each person's sales numbers through time and see who is improving."

This frequently followed charting advice could lead to Figure 2.1 report-out. Other frequent report-out formats for this type of data are shown in Figures 2.2 and 2.3.

Similar to summarizing data through a table, the chart report formats in Figures 2.1–2.3 typically lead to stories about the past. The chart presentation format will dictate the presented *story* type. For example, the calendar boundaries in the bar-chart reporting format in Figure 2.3 will surely lead to adjacent month and previous year–month comparisons. This type of chart, like the other charts, can be difficult to interpret. This interpretation difficulty often leads to inconsistencies and erroneous conclusions in the stories generated by different presenters.

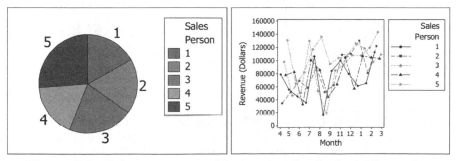

Figure 2.1: Salesperson monthly revenue for the last 12 months presented as a pie chart and line chart.

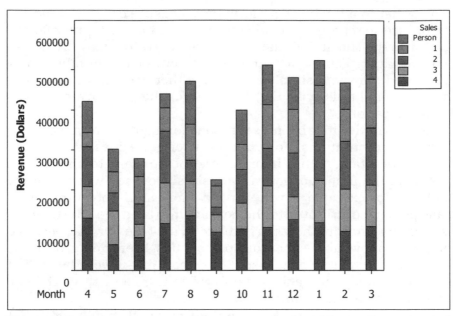

Figure 2.2: Salesperson monthly revenue for last 12 months presented as a stacked bar chart.

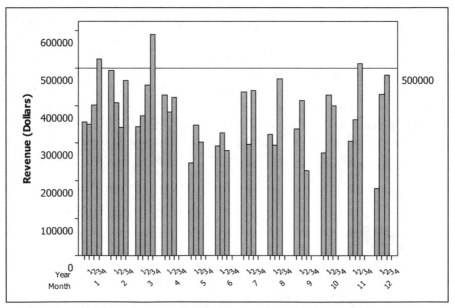

Figure 2.3: Year-to-year monthly revenue chart tracking against a mean monthly goal of $500,000. Years are designated as 0, 1, 2, and 3; for example, 0 refers to 2000 and 1 refers to 2001. The figure indicates that the data were compiled at the end of March, since there are four bars for months of 1: January, 2: February, and 3: March.

Consider which interests us the most: the past or the future? Most often the response to this question is "the future." Reporting individual up-and-down historical movement or arbitrary time-based comparisons does not provide insight to future process-output expectations, assuming that the process experiences no dramatic positive or negative change. However, if we could somehow estimate the future and didn't like the resulting prediction, we gain insight to improvement focus opportunities; that is, the metric improvement needs pull for creating a process-improvement project.

> Reporting individual up-and-down historical movement or arbitrary time-based comparisons does not provide insight to future process-output expectations.

Report charts need to lead to activities that are beneficial to the organization. Traditional tabular and chart reporting leads to *stories* about the past without any formal system that describes what might be expected in the future. Later I will discuss about the IEE alternative data-reporting system that provides increased insight as to where improvement efforts would be most beneficial.

2.4 Strategic Planning

Consider the company strategy in Figure 2.4, which typifies other companies' strategies. An organization can spend much time creating such a strategic listing; however, it can often have difficulty interpreting what it should do relative to addressing the passed-down strategy. *Integrated Enterprise Excellence – Volume 2* (Breyfogle, 2008b) describes an IEE alternative system that leads to specific actionable items with goals.

2.5 Hoshin Kanri

In Japanese, *hoshin* mean direction and shining needle (i.e. compass), while *kanri* means management. *Hoshin kanri* means management and control of the organization's direction needle, or focus. Hoshin kanri is a blending of the elements of management by objectives (MBO; Drucker, 1954) and the Deming cycle of plan–do–check–act (PDCA). A crucial job of the entire hoshin kanri decision-making theory is consistency and compatibility across all levels of management.

Foxconn's objective is to maintain its position as one of the leading manufacturers of connectors, PC enclosures, and other precision components, and to successfully develop products and market its products for use in network communication and consumer electronic products. A number of strategies have been developed to attain this objective:

Develop strategic relationship with industry leaders — By working closely with top-tier PC and IC companies, Foxconn is able to predict market trends accurately and introduce new products ahead of its competitors.

Focus on the development of global logistic capabilities — This enables Foxconn to respond quickly and efficiently to the customer's requirements around the world.

Expansion of production capacity — Foxconn currently has production facilities in Asia, Europe, and the United States. Expanding its existing production capacity increases economics of scale.

Achieve further vertical integration — Further integration of the production process allows Foxconn to exercise better control over the quality of its products.

Maintain technologically advanced and flexible production capabilities — This increases Foxconn's competitiveness relative to its peers and allows it to stay one step ahead of the opposition.

New products — Foxconn will leverage off its manufacturing expertise and continue to move tirelessly into new areas of related business.

Figure 2.4: Corporate strategry example (foxconn, 2006).

Many companies that are implementing Lean or Lean Six Sigma are also using hoshin kanri; however, implementations can vary considerably. This section provides hoshin kanri highlights, as described in Babich (2005) and Jackson (2006). *An IEE alternative will be discussed later.*

Babich (2005) describes how hoshin kanri is a system of forms and rules that provide structure for the planning process. Hoshin kanri separates the organizational plan into two parts: business fundamentals and breakthroughs. The five elements of a complete hoshin kanri plan are business-fundamentals plan, long-range plan, annual plan, review tables, and abnormality tables.

In hoshin kanri, the organization's mission should be deployed in every operational unit. Missions are generally deployed along organizational lines. A mission deployment divides the statements into lower-level essential activities to achieve the mission. When deploying an activity down one level, the activity becomes that level's mission, which can then have further segmented activities. Back and forth mission-development discussions, called catchball, involve give-and-take until consensus is reached. Each mission statement leads to the creation of a business-fundamental planning table, which contains the mission, key activities, owners, and performance measures with action limits. Table 2.2 is an example of a corporate business-fundamentals planning table.

Each activity in a business-fundamentals planning table typically has two to four performance measures (PMs) with action limits, where multiple measures are used to prevent optimizing one

Table 2.2: Hoshin kanri business-fundamentals planning table, for example (Babich, 2005). Reprinted with permission from Total Quality Engineering, Inc.

Location: Rockford International		Time Period: FY2005
Prepared By: Ira M. Cool		Date: 12/10/2004
Situation: Rockford International (RI) is a small organization supplying hardware for the building industry. Rockford specializes in designing, manufacturing, and selling hinges for cabinet doors. RI employs 130 people and has revenues of $10M. Its primary customers are Southern California custom cabinetmakers. RI's business is very volatile; it is difficult to predict when its next contract will be. When it does get a contract, however, the company wants to move very fast and can't wait for parts. Therefore, RI builds and stocks a wide variety of hinges and associated fasteners and is capable of delivering product within one day of the order. In the rare event when product is defective, RI commits to replacing the product the same day. By virtue of excellent delivery, RI charges premium prices for its products.		
Mission, based on situation:		
Mission (Owner)		**PMs (Action Limits)**
Improve the responsiveness of Southern California custom cabinetmakers by providing hinges and fasteners with one day turnaround time. (Ira)		1. % orders filled same day (<95%) 2. Revenue (<$500K/mo) 3. Profit (<6%) 4. Cust Sat (<95%)
Key Activities necessary to achieve Mission:		
Activity (Owner)		**PMs (Action Limits)**
1. Maintain Rockford International customer satisfaction by consistently shipping quality products within one day of receiving an order. (Chris)		1. Line item fill rate (< 95%) 2. Inventory (>2 mo. supply) 3. Product returns (>0.5%) 4. Units/assembler (<150K)
2. Manage Rockford International's revenue stream by supporting current customers and attracting new customers. (Bob)		1. Orders (<80% of forecast) 2. Order growth (<10%/yr) 3. Customer calls (>20/mo) 4. Sales cost (>10% of rev$)
3. Fuel Rockford International's growth by developing new products, and assure customer satisfaction by providing technical support for current products. (Jim)		1. # stop ship (>0) 2. # new products introduced per year (>10) 3. R&D cost (>10% rev$)
4. Assure Rockford International's profitability by providing information so that sound business decisions can be made. (Janet)		1. Profit (<target/mo) 2. acct receivable (>45 days) 3. Acct payable (>45 days) 4. Audit score (<95%)
5. Assure Rockford International's productivity by attracting, retaining, and training exceptional people, and assure employee satisfaction by providing a safe, comfortable, equitable, and professional working environment. (Sandy)		1. # voluntary terminations (>2/mo) 2. # complaints (>5/mo) 3. Lost work hours (>5%)

measure at the expense of the overall process health. The essence of the business-fundamentals planning table is the maintenance of performance. Tactical decisions are to be captured in the business-fundamentals planning table.

The essence of breakthrough planning is the significant improvement. Strategic decision making involves formulating the right question for the development of the long-range plan (strategic plan). Long-range planning is documented in the hoshin kanri planning table. Hoshin kanri is not to be used to figure out what to do. Hoshin kanri is a plan-implementation process that picks up where other planning processes stop. Hoshin kanri is used to help organizations deploy and execute what they want to do.

Deliverables are the tangible results of job or task completion. Gantt charts contain plots of the expected start date and completion date for each deliverable. In hoshin kanri, deliverables are associated with breakthrough plans. Breakthrough plans are formulated from the organization's vision of the future. Organizational vision translation into a long-range plan encompasses five, ten, or even twenty years, has few year-to-year changes, and has limited deployment with wide communication. The hoshin kanri annual plan table has specific long-range plan steps that are to be accomplished in the current year, keep in mind that critical-area deployment can significantly change from year to year.

The hoshin kanri form for the development and deployment of both long-range and annual plans (Table 2.3 Reprinted with permission from Total Quality Engineering, Inc.) is similar to the business-fundamentals plan table. Primary differences are the renaming of the form as Hoshin Kanri (long-range or annual) Planning Table and the replacement of the words "Mission" with "Objective," "Activities" with "Strategies," and "Action Limits" with "Goals."

In both long-range and annual hoshin kanri breakthrough plans, performance improvement is achieved through successful deliverables or tasks. Hoshin kanri annual plans should have only three or four strategies for each objective.

Similar to the business-fundamentals planning table, there is a cascading of strategies throughout the organization; that is, top level to mid level to project level. Each objective leads to the creation of a strategy that becomes the objective for the strategy creation for the next level down. This continues until specific tasks are identified and laid out in a Gantt chart.

Up to this point, discussion has focused on the planning portion of Deming's PDCA process. The Do step of PDCA can involve steps of the P-DMAIC, or design for Six Sigma *project*-execution roadmap. The Check and Act steps are hoshin kanri periodic reviews. Monthly and annual reviews can be documented in a periodic review table summary or annual plan summary review.

Hoshin kanri can become a paperwork jungle if care is not exercised. A department's hoshin kanri plan should typically consist of fewer than 12 pages: one page for business fundamentals, one page for the organization's long-range plan, one to five pages for the department's portion of the annual plan, and four quarterly review summaries.

Table 2.3: Hoshin kanri annual planning table, for example (Babich, 2005). Reprinted with permission from Total Quality Engineering, Inc.

Location: Rockford International		Time Period: FY2005	
Prepared By: Ira M. Cool		Date: 12/10/2004	
Situation: For Rockford International to achieve its long-range vision, it must expand its customer base beyond Southern California. Market research has shown that new home starts are growing faster in Spain than anywhere else in the world. Spanish contractors buy almost all of their supplies from one distributor, El Partes. El Partes only distributes material, which is at least 30% Spanish labor. The company has a reputation for distributing only high quality parts at reasonable prices. It does, however, expect large discounts from its suppliers. The Spanish government wants to encourage business and will provide tax breaks and other special incentives. If RI could distribute its parts through El Partes, RI revenue could triple in 2006 with double-digit profit. To win the El Partes contract, RI will need to establish an assembly operation in Spain, with some locally sourced material. It will also need to improve product quality and reduce operating cost.			
Key Objective, based on situation:			
Objective (Owner)		**PMs (Goals)**	
Establish a production facility in Barcelona Spain and have RI products distributed by El Partes.		1. Assembly plan operational (Q3, 05) 2. El Partes contract signed (Q4, 05) 3. Ship first hinge (1/1/06) 4. Overall project cost (<$750K)	
Key Strategies necessary to achieve Objective:			
Strategy (Owner)		**PMs (Goals)**	
1. Work with Spanish government to secure all necessary licenses and agreements. (Bob)		1. License obtained (Q1, 05) 2. Apply for Spanish grant (Q2, 05)	
2. Begin assembly operation in Spain. (Chris)		1. Building leased (Q2, 05) 2. Employees hired and trained (Q3, 05) 3. Local supplier selected (Q3, 05)	
3. Improve the quality and reliability of the 15009 hinge family. (Jim)		1. Quality (0.1% returns) 2. Mean Time Between Failures - MTBF (1 M hrs) 3. Cost (% current cost) 4. New prod Intro (Q4,05)	
4. Improve the cost structure of the RI business operations. (Ira-Staff)		1. R&D Costs (<9% rev$) 2. Sales Cost (<8% rev$) 3. Mfg Cost (<30% rev$) 4. Overhead Cost (<3% rev$)	

As noted earlier, hoshin kanri has a form-based structure. Jackson (2006) includes 36 files, most of which are in hoshin kanri forms describes the four teams and seven PDCA cycles of hoshin kanri experiments, which are nested inside each other. Experiments in this context are different from experiments described later in this book. In this context, plans become experiments, where all managers and employees conduct tests of hypothesized strategies, under standardized work control conditions.

Table 2.4: Hoshin kanri four teams and seven experiments (Jackson, 2006). Reproduced with permission. Originally published as *Hoshin Kanri for the Lean Enterprise: Developing Competitve Capabilities and Managing* by Thomas L. Jackson. Copyright © 2006 Productivity Press, an imprint of Taylor and Francis Group, an Informa Business, www.ProductivityPress.com

4 Teams			7 Experiments	
1	Hoshin Team	**1**	Long-term strategy	A general plan to action that aims over a very long period of time -- 5 to 100 years -- to make major changes or adjustments in the mission and/or vision of the business.
		2	Mid-term strategy	A partially-complete plan of action including financial targets and measures of process improvement that aims over 3 to 5 years to develop capabilities and align the trajectory of business operations with the long-term strategy.
		3	Annual hoshin	A highly concrete plan of action that aims over the next 6 to 18 months to develop competitive capabilities and align the trajectory of business operations in accordance with the midterm strategy.
2	Tactical Teams	**4**	Tactics	Concrete initiatives of 6 to 18 months, defined by the annual hoshin, undertaken to develop specific new capabilities by applying new technologies and methodologies to general business processes.
3	Operational Teams	**5**	Operations	Concrete projects of 3 to 6 months, defined by the annual hoshin, undertaken to apply new technologies and methodologies to standardized processes of specific business functions.
4	Action Team	**6**	Kaikaku	Concrete projects of 1 week to 3 months, usually defined after the deployment of the annual hoshin, undertaken to apply new tools and techniques in standardized daily work.
		7	Kaizen	Problem-solving in more or less real time to address defects, errors, and abnormalities that arise in the course of standardized daily work, as well as improvements resulting from employee suggestions.

A unique suite of documents is sometimes used to support strategic planning and problems. These documents are called A3s because in Japan they are printed on one side of European A3 paper, which is equivalent to American tabloid paper (11 × 17 in.).

Typically, nine good-project critical elements are included in these forms. These nine elements are theme (problem or challenge), problem statement, target statement (project scope), scientific process of investigation (e.g., PDCA), systematic analysis (five whys, cost benefit, cause-and-effect diagram, design of experiments, etc.), proposed solution, implementation timeline, graphical illustrations, and date and reporting unit or owner at the bottom of the form. Example A3s are intelligent report, X-matrix, team charter, status report, and problem report, where an X-matrix is used in the plan phase of the hoshin kanri process. An X-matrix can be used to bundle several A3s together for the exploration of interdependencies. Hoshin kanri tools are useful for checking market conditions as part of the *enterprise process* DMAIC, or E-DMAIC, process (Breyfogle, 2008b).

As with most things, hoshin kanri implementation has pluses and minuses. Consider the following issues that should be addressed in an implementation:

- Execution possibilities for strategies such as those shown in Table 2.4 are very team dependent and can lead to detrimental activities for the enterprise as a whole. Sections 4.1 and 4.4 provide alternative thoughts.
- The driver and infrastructure of hoshin kanri center on the cascading of executive management's strategies throughout the organization. The direction of work activity could significantly change when there is a significant change in executive leadership or leadership direction. The time could be lengthy and resource needs could be large to incorporate executive direction change into an enterprise hoshin kanri system.
- Missions and strategies are to cascade throughout the organization chart. An organizational change, company purchase, or company spin-off that redirects focus could lead to much confusion and frustration.
- For a given situation, there can be many ways to analyze data. A roadmap is needed for these analyses; for example, analyze phase of E-DMAIC.

- Table listings for performance-measure action limits can lead to the wrong activity. This format for action-limit establishment does not systematically address process shift and other situations that can be addressed only through charting. Performance-measure action limits set without examining a 30,000-foot-level control chart can lead to firefighting (see Breyfogle 2008c, for chart-creation methods).

These issues are overcome when the concepts of hoshin kanri are blended within an IEE infrastructure. Hoshin kanri techniques can be integrated into the E-DMAIC roadmap to systematically address not only the creation of projects but also day-to-day business activities (see Breyfogle 2008b).

2.6   The Balanced Scorecard

The balanced scorecard, as presented by Kaplan and Norton (1992), tracks the business in the areas of financial, customer, internal processes, and learning and growth. In this model, each area is to address one of the following questions:

- *Financial*: To succeed financially, how should we appear to our shareholders?
- Customer: To achieve our vision, how should we appear to our customers?
- *Internal business process*: To satisfy our shareholders and customers, what business processes must we excel at?
- *Learning and growth*: To achieve our vision, how will we sustain our ability to change and improve?

Figure 2.5 illustrates how these metrics are to align with the business vision and strategy. Each category is to have objectives, measures, targets, and initiatives.

Scorecard balance is important because if you don't have balance you could be giving one metric more focus than another, which can lead to problems. For example, if we only focus on-time delivery, product quality could suffer dramatically to meet ship dates. However we need to exercise care in how this balance is achieved. A natural balance is much more powerful than forcing balance through the organizational chart using a scorecard structure of financial, customer, internal business process, and learning and growth that may not be directly appropriate to all business areas. In addition, a scorecard structure that is closely tied to the

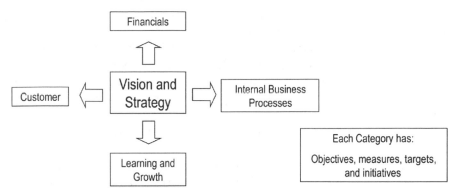

Original article: "The Balanced Scorecard – measures that drive performance," by Robert Kaplan and David Norton, 1992

Figure 2.5: Traditional performance measures: The balanced scorecard.

organization chart has an additional disadvantage in that it will need to be changed whenever significant reorganizations occur.

In IEE, we achieve natural scorecard balance throughout the business via the enterprise value chain (see Figure 7.3), noting that overall learning and growth would typically be assigned to HR but, when appropriate, can also be assigned to other functional performance. We assign metrics to the owner who is accountable for the metric's performance. These metrics can be cascaded downward to lower organization functions, where these metrics also are assigned to owners who have performance accountability. With this IEE system whenever there is an organizational change the basic value chain metrics will not change. Only the ownership will change.

When we create these metrics it is not only important to determine *what to measure* but it is also very important to also focus on the *how to report* so that this metric performance tracking leads to the most appropriate action, which may be to do nothing. Later we'll describe a system to accomplish this.

Jim Collins describes in *Good to Great* (2001) a level five leader as someone who is great while leading an organization and whose effect remains after the person is no longer affiliated with the organization. I describe the level-five-leader-created legacy as being a *Level Five System.*

> ... it seems to me that it would be very difficult for an organization to create a level five system when the primary guiding light for the organization is its strategy, which can change with new leadership.

In my workshops, I often ask, Do you think your organization's strategy would change if there were different leadership? A vast majority give a positive response to this question. Because of this, it seems to me that it would be very difficult for an organization to create a Level Five System when the primary guiding light for the organization is its strategy, which can change with new leadership.

I don't mean to imply that organizational strategies are bad, but I do believe that strategies created without structurally evaluating the overall organizational value chain and its metrics can lead to unhealthy behavior. To illustrate this, consider the following example.

Parameters for a global service corporation dashboard were defined by the following underlying strategic executive goals for the year: *grow revenue 25 percent per year, earn minimum of 20 percent net profit, achieve 60 percent of revenue with repeat customers, balance regional growth, fill open positions corresponding with growth, ensure that all employees are competent and high performers, realize projects within time and cost targets, limit ratio of overhead to productive time to 20 percent, and satisfy customers 100 percent.*

These objectives, measures, targets, and initiatives were then set up to be monitored, as shown in Figure 2.6, where each metric is to have an owner. Color-coding is used to help clearly identify actual performance versus targets and forecasts. The exclamation marks indicate red flags, where objectives are not being met and attention is needed.

These executive dashboard metrics can then be drilled down further, as shown in Figure 2.7. Would you like to sign up to own this metric and its achievement? The strategic objectives described previously set a customer-satisfaction metric goal of 100 percent. Not a bad target; however, meeting this number is not easy. Simply setting this goal will not make it happen, at least not as the team setting the goal would like it to happen. One might wonder how this goal was determined. Do you think this goal is SMART; that is, specific, measurable, actionable, relevant, time-based?

For this metric type, an unachieved goal earns an exclamation mark, indicating that the metric's owner may need reminding that his or her job-performance rating depends on achievement of this goal. What kind of activity might this type of pressure create, especially when improvement detection is immediately needed? We might initially think that the owner would, as soon as possible,

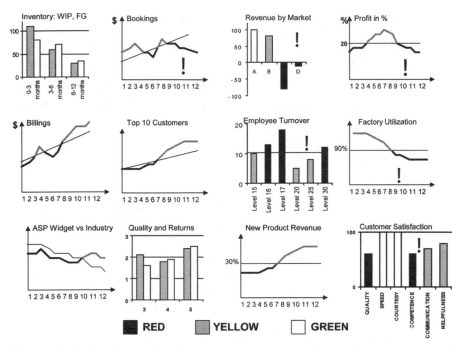

Figure 2.6: Traditional performance measures: The balanced scorecard executive dashboard. WIP: Work in progress, FG: finished goods

start an investigation into where quality improvements need to be made. But we need to be realistic. Immediate improvements are needed to make this scorecard look better. Might there be other ways to make this happen?

Before we react, let's step back to see the bigger picture. A customer-satisfaction goal is not being met; however, is this level of customer satisfaction really a problem? What were the scores from previous reporting periods? If the scores are better now, this would be good since improvements are being demonstrated, even though the strategic goal is not being met. Without a historical time-dependent reference, could there be disagreements for what is good or bad?

Keeping in mind the type of metric described in Figure 2.7, consider the following situation:

A few years ago, when my wife and I were buying a new car, negotiating the price of the car with the sales associate got to be a game with me. After we closed the deal, the sales associate pointed to a survey that was facing us under his Plexiglas desktop. This survey had all

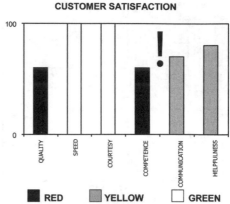

**EXECUTIVE DASHBOARD
CUSTOMER SATISFACTION EXAMPLE**

What do you measure?
Customer satisfaction summarizes your customer's rating of your products and services along industry specific parameters. General criteria are quality, delivery, service, and price.

How do you measure?
Customer ratings are standardized and quantified

Where do you find the data?
You always have to ask the customer. There is no "internal" customer satisfaction measurement that objectively reflects the customer's voice. Gathering data can reach from calling your customers with a prepared questionnaire, or collecting scorecards from customers, to engaging customer survey experts.

Figure 2.7: Traditional performance measures: The balanced scorecard/dashboard customer satisfaction drill-down.

5s checked. He told us that we would be getting a survey in the mail. Then he said that he always gets 5s on his survey. He pointed to my wife and said that he wanted her, not me, to fill out the survey.

Consider the following points:

- The salesman said we would receive a survey in the mail.
- He pointed out that he always gets 5s, as noted on the survey form on his desk.
- He wanted my wife, not me, to fill out the survey.

Do you think he might be trying to bias the survey in his favor, perhaps a bonus is riding on these results? Do you think this type of behavior is what the metric should be creating? This is one form of trying to manage the output of the metric process, rather than systematically working to change the process, or the inputs to the process, so that an improved response occurs. Simply setting high-level goals and then managing to those goals can lead to the wrong behavior. Making true long-lasting gains in customer satisfaction is more involved than working to get satisfactory scores on evaluation sheets. Attaining long-lasting customer satisfaction involves improving the process and the inputs to the process.

Let's next examine the profit scorecard in Figure 2.8. Notice that the x-axis units are 1–12. What do you think this indicates? Months is a good bet since the metric starts with 1, which is probably the first month after the company's fiscal year. Notice, also, how this tracking is made only against the goal with no indication of what kind of performance has been experienced in

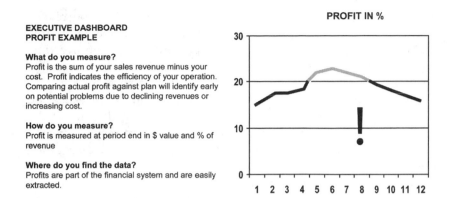

**EXECUTIVE DASHBOARD
PROFIT EXAMPLE**

What do you measure?
Profit is the sum of your sales revenue minus your cost. Profit indicates the efficiency of your operation. Comparing actual profit against plan will identify early on potential problems due to declining revenues or increasing cost.

How do you measure?
Profit is measured at period end in $ value and % of revenue

Where do you find the data?
Profits are part of the financial system and are easily extracted.

Figure 2.8: Traditional performance measures: The balanced scorecard/dashboard profit drill-down.

the past. Since the goals are annualized, the target line is drawn beginning the first month of the year, but there is no record of performance the previous year, or whether the goal is reasonable or simply a pie-in-the-sky objective.

If people are really held accountable for achieving this metric objective, very undesirable behavior can result. Since there is an exclamation point, the owner of this metric would need to take immediate action to drive these numbers in the right direction. A high-level metric such as this could lead to the Enron effect, where money could be simply shifted from one area to the next to make things look better; Or the metric could lead to immediate cost-cutting measures that might significantly damage the company's future outlook. You can cost cut your into profitability for only so long. At some point in time you will see diminishing returns and possible increase in fixed costs due to inefficiencies created by the lack of resources. This form of metric reporting can also lead to the previously described behavior, where Krispy Kreme shipped donuts that they knew would be returned so that quarterly expectations would be met.

Metric reporting, where focus is given only to whether output-type goals are met, can cause behavioral problems lower in the organization as well. Consider the following:

A prison representative purchased a commodity item only at the end of the supplier's quarterly financial reporting period. Near the end of every quarter, the salesperson for the supplier called, offering the prison a price incentive for immediate purchase. Because of the type of product sold, there was no reason for this cyclic behavior. Since manufacturing personnel were on overtime and were under pressure to increase production volume, quality problems were more prevalent during this period than others.

This odd behavior was eventually noticed and an investigation was conducted. Asked why the prison waited until the end of the quarter to purchase the product, the representative responded that the salesperson called at the end of the quarter with the discounted price.

Additional company investigation revealed that the salesperson typically had difficulty in meeting his quarterly target objective. Near the end of every quarter, the salesperson would ask his manager for approval to give customer discounts, which would help their department meet its targeted goals. If these goals were not met, there would be no personal or departmental bonuses. The manager routinely complied.

What makes this situation even worse is that the salesperson was getting paid off the top line (total products sold), while the company was taking a significant impact at the bottom line. That is, the salesperson was getting rewarded for total products sold, while the company's true profit from the transaction was reduced by the sales commission as well as additional overtime costs due to demand spike.

All these negative corporate-profitability behaviors originated with the company's salesperson commission policy. Rather than someone noticing and investigating, this type of situation could be readily identified in an E-DMAIC structure during the analyze phase. In this structure, a project could have been created that later resolved the undesirable behavior of the sales department through changing either the reward policy or the discounting policy so that these demand spikes would no longer occur.

The shortcomings of many traditional performance metrics are that they often reflect only fiscal year metrics, make comparisons to a point estimate from a previous month or year, and don't have a procedure for improving the process so that gains occur and are maintained. These traditional methods don't view the enterprise process as a system of processes, where the performance metric is the result of these processes along with the variability that occurs within them. Long-lasting change is a result of systematic improvement to these processes.

> The shortcomings of many traditional performance metrics are that these metrics often reflect only fiscal year metrics, make comparisons to a point estimate from a previous month or a previous year, and don't have a procedure for improving the process so that gains occur and are maintained.

This form of metric reporting is always after-the-fact reporting and not predictive. Imagine if a customer said, "Based on past experience, our products will have a consumer half-life of only – years. If innovations and improvements are not sustained, our revenues will decline by – percent over the next – years." This type of data-driven statement leads to long-term thinking that can have long-lasting results.

2.7   Red–Yellow–Green Scorecards

The previously described balance scorecards and other scorecards that are not balanced often use red, yellow, and green to show whether actions are needed relative to meeting established objectives. The Office of Planning and Performance Management of the U.S. Department of Interior uses these metrics in the following way (U.S. Dept. of Interior, 2003):

> Office of Management and Budget (OMB) has established an Executive Branch Management Scorecard to track how well departments and agencies are executing the five President's Management Agenda (PMA) components. The Scorecard also strengthens the sense of accountability on the part of these agencies. The Scorecard presents an updated assessment of the status and progress being made to address each of the President's Management Agenda (PMA) goals.
>
> Status is assessed against the standards for success that have been developed for each initiative and are published in the 2003 Budget. They are defined as follows:
>
> - Green: Meets all of the standards for success.
> - Yellow: Achieved some, but not all, of the criteria.
> - Red: Has any one of a number of serious flaws.

Progress is assessed on a case-by-case basis against the deliverables and timelines that each agency has established for the five PMA components. They are defined as:

- Green: Implementation is proceeding according to plans.
- Yellow: Some slippage or other issues requiring adjustment by the agency in order to achieve the initiative objectives in a timely manner.
- Red: Initiative [is] in serious jeopardy and is unlikely to realize objectives absent significant management intervention.

The President reviews each agency scorecard with the respective cabinet member.

Interior is using the Scorecard approach to assist in monitoring progress toward achieving the PMA goals at a departmental level. Criteria specific to Interior and its bureaus were developed through a collaborative, cross-departmental effort. The criteria were combined with rating scales from 0 to 10 using color rating bars that visually indicate progress and status scores. Interior bureaus and offices are asked to conduct a self-assessment of their status and progress in realizing PMA goals every six months, with the first of these self-assessments conducted in May 2002. Based on the self-assessment, the Department identifies the next actions that need to be taken by specific bureaus and offices to "get to green." Actions are entered into the Department's PMA tracking system so that they can be monitored along with the Citizen-Centered Governance Plan activities to assess the Department's progress as a whole in meeting the PMA goals.

When it is conducted throughout an organization, do you think that this form of goal setting and managing to these goals will lead to the right behavior? Goals are important; however, metric targets need to be SMART (see Glossary). Arbitrary goal setting and management to these goals can lead to the wrong behavior!

Let's now discuss the presentation of red–yellow–green scorecards, which can have different presentation formats. Figure 2.9 and Table 2.5 illustrate two possible formats.

Let's further examine a scorecard like Table 2.5. When creating this type of scorecard, metrics are established throughout the organization, along with goals for the metrics. When a metric goal is being met, all is well and the color is green. When measurements are close to not being met, the color is yellow. The metric is colored red when the goal is not being met and corrective action needs to be taken.

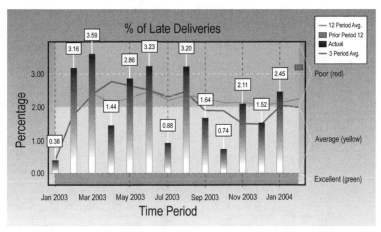

Figure 2.9: Red–yellow–green graphical reporting.

What do you see in this scorecard? There are a lot of metrics grouped by business area. Also, many measurements are colored red and metrics even transition from red to green and back. Finally, there are a lot of metrics for one scorecard. One rule of thumb is that most scorecards should include 7–10 metrics. Any more than that and a person will struggle monitoring and acting on them.

How can you have a metric that is red for the entire reporting period? Is no one monitoring it? Is it based on an arbitrary target and just ignored? We don't know, but all are possible.

Since red–yellow–green scorecard reporting is now readily available on many ERP systems, cascading this type of scorecard throughout the organization can initially seem very appealing. However, with this form of reporting, some companies might be experiencing many, if not all, green metrics. While in other companies red-triggered events can be creating a lot of work; however, when the metrics are examined collectively over time there does not seem to be much, if any, individual metric improvement.

When assessing these two types of company scorecard situations, one might think that there would be a big difference in how well the organizations are performing. However, this is not necessarily true.

Perhaps the first company is a supplier to a company or government agency that requires red–yellow–green scorecard reporting and includes in their agreement a penalty if the color is not green. What kind of goal-setting activity would result

Table 2.5: Red-yellow–green tabular scorecard example.

RED

YELLOW

GREEN

Monthly SCORECARD
Business Unit Name

Measurement	Targets	Aug'04	Sep'04	Oct'04	Nov'04	Dec'04
FINANCE						
Finance Metric A		3.387525	2.965966	3.042505	2.891057	3.485847
Yellow if equal to or higher than	3.05	3.05	3.05	3.05	3.05	3.05
Green if equal to or higher than	3.1	3.1	3.1	3.1	3.1	3.1
Finance Metric B		2.09819	2.254758	2.345674	2.207099	2.316309
Yellow if equal to or higher than	2.2	2.2	2.2	2.2	2.2	2.2
Green if equal to or higher than	2.25	2.25	2.25	2.25	2.25	2.25
Finance Metric C		0.762611	0.958071	1.051227	0.867969	1.158351
Yellow if equal to or higher than	0.9	0.9	0.9	0.9	0.9	0.9
Green if equal to or higher than	0.95	0.95	0.95	0.95	0.95	0.95

CUSTOMER

FINANCE

INTERNAL BUSINESS OPS

LEARNING & GROWTH

from this type of policy, especially if the customer is not actively involved in all goal-setting metrics?

People in the second organization are expending a lot of effort trying to improve their many metrics when they are red. It would seem that these organizations might start lobbying for lower goals when they are set for the next fiscal year.

How well red–yellow–green scorecards are performing depends on the established goals, which may not realistic and/or lead process suboptimization effort throughout the organization chart. Metric tracking against this type of goals can lead to ineffective firefighting activities or playing games with the numbers.

Game playing to meet calendar goals can also impact bonuses. This form of activity can occur not only in the sales department but also at the executive level. The following example illustrates how the wrong activity can be stimulated at an employee level by a goal-driven metric.

> This company's business service involved managing large amounts of customer money. Large checks could flow to the company from its customer even though the company kept only a small portion of the money. All employees in a company were given bonus if they met the calendar-based revenue. A company goal had been set at one level for many years, so employees became accustomed to receiving this periodic bonus compensation.
>
> A major customer was to make an unusually large payment. The payment size required signature approval by the customer's CEO. The customer asked if they could pay in smaller amounts spread over a longer period so they could avoid the hassle of having CEO approval. The service company agreed since it wanted to be customer-driven but later determined that this agreement negated the periodic bonus.
>
> In an attempt to resolve this employee-bonus unfairness, an administrator took it upon himself to adjust the compensation internally so it appeared that the company was paid in the period the service was performed. However, this accounting adjustment negatively impacted the customer and caused havoc.

Have you experienced any organization that has had similar issues with a goal-driven metric? A final example follows:

> A salesperson calls customers who have committed to purchasing products in the next quarter, asking them if they would move up their order to the current quarter. He then offers a discount for this order shift. The salesperson's motivation for doing this was that he

was having trouble meeting his quarterly numbers, which would negatively impact his pay for this quarter. The consequence of this practice is similar to the previous illustration.

Employee incentive plans are not bad; however, care needs to be exercised or the wrong activities can prevail. An alternative scorecard style to red–yellow–green metrics is described in Examples 7.1–7.4.

2.8 Stimulating the Right Behavior

This chapter described how traditional metric presentation formats can often be deceiving and not lead to the best actions for the business as a whole. The next chapter describes how organizations can overcome these issues and stimulate the right behavior through IEE.

3

Improving Management Governance and Innovation through IEE

The previous chapter described the problems with traditional business metrics and how conventional strategic planning can lead to activities that are not in the best interest of the business as a whole. This chapter provides a high-level description of how

> IEE can create a culture that transitions organizations from firefighting to an orchestrated system that moves toward the three Rs of business.

Integrated Enterprise Excellence (IEE) can create a culture that transition of organizations from firefighting to an orchestrated governance system that moves toward the three Rs of business: everyone doing the Right things and doing them Right at the Right time.

In a company the governance model might define the composition of the cross-organizational or cross-functional teams who will monitor the processes, the metrics, the meeting frequency, and so on. Organizations can have governance models for key strategic areas like total customer experience, warranty, and so on. Rather than targeting key strategies, which can change over time, the IEE system focus is on the enterprise value chain, its metrics, and targeted improvement efforts. The overall governance system for this focus can be achieved through E-DMAIC, which can be orchestrated by the enterprise process management (EPM) organization (see Breyfogle, 2008b).

As business competition gets tougher, there is much pressure on product development, manufacturing, and service organizations to become more productive and efficient. Developers need to create innovative products in less time, even though the products may be more complex. Manufacturing organizations feel growing pressure to improve quality while decreasing costs and to increase production volumes with fewer resources. Service organizations must reduce lead times and improve customer satisfaction. Organizations can address these issues by adopting an implementation strategy that has direct linkage to both customer needs and bottom-line benefits. One might summarize this process as the following:

> IEE is a sustainable business management governance system, which integrates business scorecards, strategies, and process improvement so that organizations move toward the three Rs of business (everyone is doing the Right things and doing them Right at the Right time). IEE provides the framework for innovation and continual improvement, which goes beyond Lean Six Sigma's project-based defect- and waste-reduction methods. The existence and excellence of a business depends more on customers and cash; or, $E = MC^2$. As a business way of life, IEE provides the organizational orchestration to achieve more customer and cash.

The word *quality* often carries excess baggage with some people and therefore does not appear in this definition. For example, it is often difficult to get buy in throughout an organization when a program is viewed as a quality program that is run by the quality department. IEE should be viewed as a methodology that applies to all functions within every organization. This system can become the framework for overcoming communication barriers and building an organizational cultural norm for continuous improvement. The wise application of statistical and nonstatistical tools, including business metrics such as satellite-level and 30,000-foot-level metrics, occurs at all levels. Organizations benefit considerably when these scorecard/dashboard metrics and improvement techniques become a business way of life; however, there can be initial resistance to adopting the overall system.

The performance and improvement system of IEE basically lowers the water level in an organization, which can expose some ugly rocks. People who have been hiding behind an ineffective organizational measurement and improvement system could initially be very concern by the increased visibility to their functional performance. However, an advantage of the IEE system is that the system not only can show ugly rocks but also has a very effective step-by-step system for remove the rocks – one by one starting with the largest rocks first.

3.1 Overview of IEE

Management must ask the right questions; the right questions lead to the wise use of statistical and nonstatistical techniques for the purpose of obtaining knowledge from facts and data. Management needs to encourage the *wise* application of statistical techniques. Management needs to operate using the bromide In God we trust; all others bring data.

This book suggests periodic process reviews and projects based on assessments leading to a knowledge-centered activity (KCA) focus in all aspects of the business, where KCA describes efforts for wisely obtaining knowledge and then wisely using this knowledge within the organizations and processes. KCA can redirect the focus of business so that efforts are more productive.

When implemented at GE, Six Sigma had evolved to a project-based system, where emphasis was given to defect reduction. In this deployment, the quantification of project success was an improved process sigma quality level (see Glossary for sigma quality level definition) and with a quantifiable financial benefit (Breyfogle, 2008c).

Because Six Sigma projects begin with a problem statement, it is only natural that Six Sigma is considered to be a problem-solving system. The evolution from Six Sigma to Lean Six Sigma resulted in the expansion of problem statement opportunities to include the gambit of considering waste in traditional Lean deployments; that is, overproduction, waiting, transportation, inventory, over-processing, motion, defects, and people utilization.

However, often project deployments that center on the use of Lean or Six Sigma tools do not significantly impact the organization's big picture. Organizations may not pick the best projects to work on, which could result in suboptimization that makes the system as a whole worse. In addition, Lean Six Sigma is a project-driven system, not a business system. IEE is an encompassing business system that addresses these issues, and more.

Lean Six Sigma curriculums typically don't address organizational measurements and the building of a business strategy that targets the system as a whole. Define–measure–analyze–improve–control (DMAIC) is the traditional roadmap for executing and managing Six Sigma process-improvement projects. DMAIC is used in IEE not only to describe process-improvement project execution steps, but also to establish the framework for the overall enterprise process.

Figure 3.1 shows how the IEE *enterprise process* DMAIC roadmap has linkage in the *enterprise process* improve phase to the *improvement project* DMAIC roadmap and *design project* define–measure–analyze–design–verify (DMADV) roadmap. The measure phase of the improvement project DMAIC roadmap has the additional noted drill-downs.

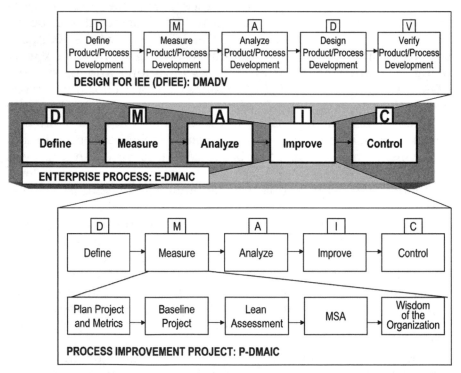

Figure 3.1: IEE high-level enterprise process roadmap with P-DMAIC process improvement and DMADV design project roadmaps (MSA: measurement systems analysis).

I refer to the enterprise-process DMAIC roadmap as E-DMAIC and to the project P-DMAIC

As noted earlier, I refer to the enterprise-process DMAIC roadmap as E-DMAIC and to the project DMAIC roadmap as P-DMAIC. The high-level P-DMAIC project-execution roadmap steps are shown in Breyfogle (2008c).

Figure 3.2 illustrates the IEE integration of Lean, Six Sigma, and other tools and techniques in both the enterprise and process-improvement project level. In the E-DMAIC roadmap, Lean tools are specifically described in the analyze phase. In the P-DMAIC roadmap, Lean tools are specifically described in the measure and improve phases.

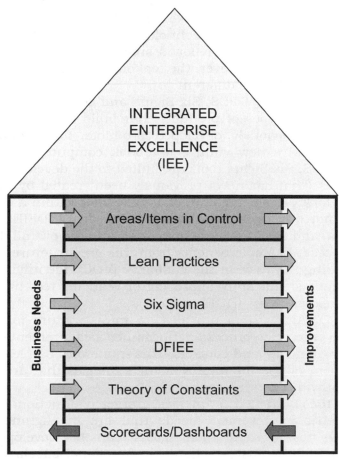

Figure 3.2: Integration of tools and methodologies.

Excessive measurement-system error can lead to firefighting behavior and makes it difficult to develop the correlations that help determine what inputs drive the outputs. The focus tends to be on improving the process, when the needed effort should be on improving the measurement systems. Measurement systems analysis (MSA) addresses these issues, which are applicable as both enterprise performance metrics and project metrics (see Breyfogle, 2008c).

There are execution steps to walk-through for the organization's enterprise-process (E-DMAIC) and process-improvement project (P-DMAIC) roadmap (Breyfogle, 2008c). Many Six Sigma and Lean tools are also applied to the design-project DMADV process, which is often called design for Six Sigma (DFSS) or design for Lean Six Sigma (DFLSS). In IEE this design system is sometimes called design for Integrated Enterprise Excellence, or DFIEE.

DFIEE/DFSS projects can take the form of product design, process design, or information technology (IT) projects. In IEE these three DFIEE/DFSS forms follow a similar DMADV roadmap, as noted in Figure 3.1; however, the tool emphasis for each of these situations can be quite different.

In product DFIEE/DFSS, Six Sigma and Lean tools are linked to address new types of products that build on the knowledge gained from previously developed products, for example, the development of a new vintage notebook computer. In process DFIEE/DFSS, Six Sigma tools are linked to the development of a new process that has never previously been created by the organization, for example, creation of a call center within a company that did not previously have a call center. In IT, DFIEE/DFSS, Six Sigma, and Lean tools are integrated into the overall development process. Example benefits from this are structure systems for capturing the voice of the customer (VOC), identifying risks, and perhaps significantly improving or reducing test times with design of experiments (DOE) strategies.

The E-DMAIC system provides an infrastructure for linking high-level enterprise-process-performance measurements, analyses, improvements, and controls. This framework can lead to the development of specific improvement strategies that are in true alignment with business goals.

From these created strategies, targeted functional value-chain metric improvement needs that are in alignment with these business measurement goals can be developed (see Breyfogle, 2008b). Positive change in functional-baseline performance scorecard/dashboard metrics at the 30,000-foot-level is the measure of success relative to achieving targets. Each functional business-measurement goal is to have an owner whose personal performance is measured against achieving the relevant metric goal.

Long-lasting improvements in the 30,000-foot-level scorecard/dashboard metrics are the result of systematic process-improvement and design projects. This IEE improvement-metric system creates a stimulus that results in a pull for project creation. From this system, projects are created that are in true alignment to business needs. In addition, this system framework leads to the creation and execution of a long-lasting business-measurement and business-improvement organizational system.

This system can provide many more benefits than the push for Lean Six Sigma project creation from a list of potential projects and the execution of these projects, where the primary quantification of success is the amount of money saved. In addition, these projects might not have true alignment to business needs.

IEE's execution flow follows the overall thought process of evaluating the enterprise process (E-DMAIC) to the mechanics of executing a specific improvement project (P-DMAIC), as illustrated in Figure 3.1. Breyfogle (2008c) provides highlights of the benefits of Six Sigma and Lean tools that are most applicable and that challenge some of the traditional Six Sigma and Lean Six Sigma techniques that can lead to questionable results. I will expand on other techniques that are beyond the boundaries of these methodologies. The reader can refer to *Implementing Six Sigma* (Breyfogle, 2003) for elaboration on the traditional methodologies of Six Sigma and Lean.

> It has been my observation that many Six Sigma and Lean Six Sigma implementations have a push for a project creation system. This can lead to projects that have little, if any, value to the true bottom line of the organization or to multiple projects claiming the same savings.

It has been my observation that many Six Sigma and Lean Six Sigma implementations have a push for a project creation system. This can lead to projects that have little, if any, value to the true bottom line of the organization or to multiple projects claiming the same savings.

The described approach in this book goes beyond traditional techniques, so that there is a pull for project creation by enterprise-process measurements. A traditional Six Sigma model can lead to all levels of management asking for the creation of Six

Sigma projects that improve the numbers against which they are measured. These projects often are not as beneficial as one might think, since this project-selection approach does not focus on identifying and resolving enterprise-process constraint issues. We have had people come back to us saying that another Six Sigma provider is claiming that they have saved 100 million dollars in a company; however, no one can seem to find the money.

The IEE approach can help sustain Six Sigma or Lean Six Sigma activities, a problem that many companies that have previously implemented Six Sigma or Lean Six Sigma are now confronting. In addition, this system focuses on downplaying a traditional Six Sigma policy that all Six Sigma projects must have a defined defect. I have found that this policy can lead to many nonproductive activities, game playing with the numbers, and overall frustration. The practice of not defining a defect makes this strategy much more conducive to a true integration with general workflow-improvement tools that use Lean thinking methods.

Various steps have been proposed by organizations while executing Six Sigma. Motorola frequently referenced a six-step approach to implementing Six Sigma. I referenced a ten-step Motorola approach in *Statistical Methods for Testing Development and Manufacturing* (Breyfogle, 1992b), which I preferred over Motorola's more frequently referenced six-step approach, since the ten-step method linked the steps with statistical and nonstatistical application tools.

To achieve success, organizations must wisely address metrics and their infrastructure. The success of deployment is linked to a set of cross-functional metrics that lead to significant improvements in customer satisfaction and bottom-line benefits. Companies experiencing success have created an infrastructure that supports this strategy.

An IEE business strategy involves the measurement of how well business processes meet organizational goals and offers strategies to make needed improvements. The application of the techniques to all functions results in a very high level of quality at reduced costs with a reduction in lead times, resulting in improved profitability and a competitive advantage. It is most important to choose the best set of measurements for a particular situation and to focus on the wise integration of statistical and other improvement tools offered by an IEE implementation.

A mission of Six Sigma is the reduction of cost of poor quality (COPQ). Traditionally, the broad costing categories of COPQ are internal failure costs, external failure costs, appraisal costs, and prevention costs. In Six Sigma, COPQ has a less rigid interpretation and perhaps a broader scope. In Six Sigma, COPQ means not doing what is right the first time, which can encompass anything from scrap to reworks to meetings with no purpose. COPQ also encompasses the cost of process steps that do not add value to a product or service for which a customer is willing to pay. In this book, I prefer to reference this metric as the cost of doing nothing differently (CODND). CODND has broader cost implications than COPQ, which could be perceived as a quality initiative.

Quality cost issues can dramatically affect a business, but very important ones are often hidden from view. Organizations can be missing the largest issues when they focus only on the tip of the iceberg, as shown in Figure 3.3. It is important for the organizations to direct their efforts, so these hidden issues, which are often more important than the readily visible ones, are uncovered. IEE techniques can help flatten many of the issues that affect overall cost. However, management must ask the right questions before these issues are addressed effectively. Success is the function of a need, a vision, and a plan.

This book describes the IEE business strategy: executive ownership, a support infrastructure, projects with bottom-line results, full-time (suggested) black belts, part-time green belts, reward

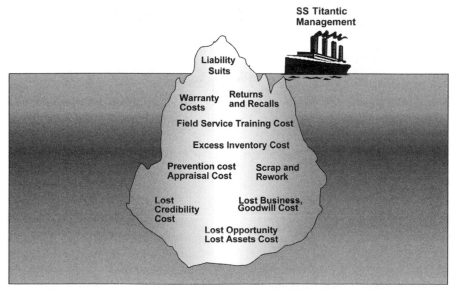

Figure 3.3: Cost of poor quality, or cost of doing nothing differently (CODND).

and motivation considerations, finance engagement (i.e., to determine the CODND and return on investment for projects), and training in all roles, both "hard" and "soft" skills.

Organizations create strategic plans and policies. They also create goals that describe the intent of the organization. These goals should have measurable results, which are attained through defined action plans. The question of concern is: How effective and aligned are these management-system practices within an organization? An improvement to this system can dramatically impact an organization's bottom line.

An IEE system measures the overall organization using scorecard/dashboard metrics which report at the satellite-level and 30,000-foot-level metrics, as illustrated in Figure 3.4. Physically, these metrics can have many forms, as illustrated in Figure 3.5. Traditional business metrics that could be classified as satellite-level metrics are gross revenue; profit; net profit margin; earnings before interest, depreciation, and amortization (EBIDA); and VOC. Traditional operational metrics at the 30,000-foot-level are defective or defect rates, lead time, waste, days sales outstanding

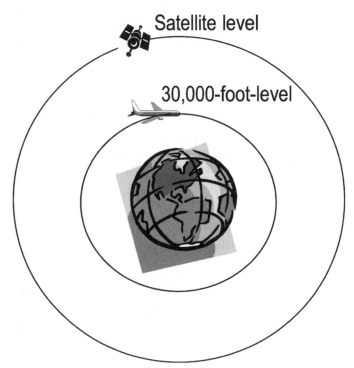

Figure 3.4: Satellite-level and 30,000-foot-level
scorecard/dashboard metrics.

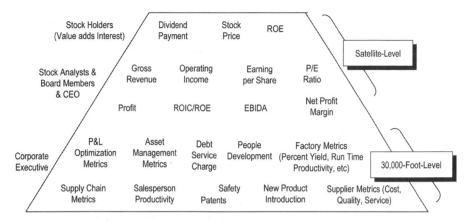

ROE = Return on Equity; OI = Operating Income; P/E = Price to Earnings; ROIC = Return on Invested Capital
P&L = Profit & Loss; EBIDA = Earnings Before Interest Depreciation, and Amortization; VOC = Voice of the Customer

Figure 3.5: Example satellite-level and 30,000-foot-level metrics.

(DSO), on-time delivery, number of days from promise date, number of days from customer-requested date, dimensional property, inventory, and head count. The enterprise-process financial analysis can be linked to these metrics, leading to process-improvement projects (Breyfogle, 2008b).

Both satellite-level and 30,000-foot-level metrics are tracked over time and are not bounded by calendar year. If nothing has changed in ten years, satellite-level and 30,000-foot-level charts would present how the system performed over the past ten years. Organizations will find it very beneficial when they align

> Both satellite-level and 30,000-foot-level metrics are tracked over time and are not bounded by calendar year. If nothing has changed in ten years, satellite-level and 30,000-foot-level charts would present how the system performed over the past ten years.

project selection with satellite-level measures from theory of constraint (TOC) metrics; that is, TOC throughput (see Glossary), investment and inventory, and operating expense.

Data presented in the satellite-level and 30,000-foot-level scorecard/dashboard format provide additional business insight when, for example, compared to tabular quarterly format reporting. Satellite-level and 30,000-foot-level reporting involves the creation of scorecard/dashboard metrics throughout the organization's value chain. An enterprise cascading-measurement methodology

> Key Process Output Variable – an important measurable process response

(ECMM) is a system that cascades and aligns important metrics throughout the organization, so that meaningful measurements are statistically tracked over time at various functional levels of the business.

ECMM tracking cascades satellite-level business metrics down to high-level key process output variables (KPOV) operational metrics. These high-level KPOV metrics might have a 30,000-foot-level, 20,000-foot-level, and 10,000-foot-level metric reporting, where all these high-level metrics are tracked using infrequent subgrouping/sampling techniques. This cascading can further progress down to 50-foot-level key process input variable (KPIV) metrics, where frequent sampling feedback is used to determine when timely adjustments are needed to a process.

High-level KPOV metrics provide voice of the process (VOP) views at various organizational levels, while low-level KPIV metrics provide the trigger when timely process-adjustments are needed, so that high-level KPOV performance is maintained. For example, in popular grocery stores, a high-level KPOV cascaded metric from an overall customer satisfaction metric could be grocery store check-out time. A related low-level KPIV to this high-level check-out-time metric would be the number of people in line, which could provide a timely decision point for determining whether grocery store checkers should be added, reduced, or remain the same.

High-level ECMM metrics in conjunction with an effective process improvement system can transition a business from a culture of firefighting to one of fire prevention. Within this fire-prevention culture, business performance metric improvement

> KPIV: Key Process Input Variable – a process input that can significantly affect its response.

needs pull for the creation of projects that lead to long-lasting, beneficial process change. The result from this is that there are less future fires to fight.

An illustration of how an organizational metric cascading environment can create a fire-prevention culture is as follows:

An enterprise's 30,000-foot-level on-time-shipment tracking could consist of weekly random selecting 100 product shipments and then comparing how well each shipment performed relative to its due date. For this reporting, each product shipment could be viewed as an attribute; that is, it was received on time or not. This data would then be combined to create a weekly cumulated nonconformance rate for deliveries relative to due dates.

For this reporting format, a shipment that is one day late would carry the same delinquency severity level as a shipment that is twenty days late. Typically the reporting of these two non-compliance deliveries would not be viewed with an equivalent level of dissatisfaction. Hence, if at all possible, it would be better to convert this form of attribute conformance reporting to continuous data, for example, a 3.0 would indicate three days late, while –1.0 would indicate one day early.

This data format could then be tracked over time using the basic IEE scorecard/dashboard metric reporting process described below. There should be ownership for each 30,000-foot-level metric. This owner would be responsible for achieving assigned future process improvement goals for his/her 30,000-foot-level performance metric(s).

During an E-DMAIC study, this metric could have been determined to be a high potential area for improvement. This volume will later show how an enterprise improvement plan (EIP) can be used to drill down from a goal to high potential areas for improvement.

This 30,000-foot-level metric could also be cascaded downward as a 20,000-foot-level metric, 10,000-foot-level metric, etc. throughout the organization. This could be accomplished by using a similar sampling procedure to the one described above for product delivery times by sites and perhaps individual part numbers. The assignment of deliver metric ownership for the 20,000-foot-level and other components of the 30,000-foot-level organizational metrics can provide the focus needed for process measurement and improvement opportunities.

If an improvement is desired for this enterprise 30,000-foot-level metric, a Pareto chart could be useful to determine which sites and part numbers should be given focus for improving the 30,000-foot-level metric as a whole; that is, the creation of targeted projects that are pulled for creation by metric improvement needs.

The reader should note how this approach is quite different than passing down an across the board goal of "improving on-time shipments" for all sites through an organizational chart or other means. With the above approach, sites that are performing well need to only maintain their performance, while other sites that are not performing well would get the needed attention focus for determining what to do to improve their performance. In the sites that are not doing well, one or more projects would be pulled for creation by this metric improvement need.

> **NONCONFORMANCE: Failure to meet a specification**

This individual-measurement report tracking is accomplished through the metric-reporting process for the IEE scorecard/dashboard as follows:

1. Assess process predictability.
2. When the process is considered predictable, formulate a prediction statement for the latest region of stability. The usual reporting format for this prediction statement is the following:
   a. When there is a specification requirement: nonconformance percentage or defects per million opportunities (DPMO).
   b. When there is no specification requirement: median response and 80 percent frequency of occurrence rate.

In IEE, prediction statements are referred to as a process capability/performance metric. If there is a specification or requirement, IEE prediction statements usually are reported as a nonconformance proportion rate, for example, out-of-specification percentage or DPMO. In IEE both continuous and attribute pass or fail response data use this reporting format. If there are no specifications or requirements for a continuous response, then a median response and 80 percent frequency of occurrence rate is reported. An 80 percent frequency of occurrence rate is typically used for this situation, since this percentage provides an easy-to-understand picture of the variability around the median that can be expected from the process.

It needs to be highlighted that prediction statements provide a best estimate of how the process is currently performing and what performance could be expected from the process in the future, unless something changes. Predictive processes can shift either positively or negatively at any time, in any month or day of the year. When a process shifts between two stable and predictable regions, the quantification of the before-and-after change (predictive statements difference) is a best-estimate statement for the project's benefit.

This metric-tracking approach assesses the organization as a system, which can lead to focused improvement efforts and a reduction of firefighting activities. Data presented in this format can be useful for executives as an input to the creation of strategic plans and then for tracking the results from the execution of those plans. With this strategy, action plans to achieve organizational goals center on the creation and implementation of projects in the E-DMAIC system, as illustrated in Figure 3.6.

The following describes the basic thought process of an E-DMAIC execution using the steps of Figure 3.6.

Step 1 (Define phase of E-DMAIC)
- Define vision and mission.

Step 2 (Define phase [value chain steps] and measure phase [value chain measurements] of E-DMAIC).
- Describe value chain, including 30,000-foot-level metrics.
- Create satellite-level metrics for the past three to ten years. We want to ensure that the selected time is long enough that multiple business cycles are captured.
- Compile 30,000-foot-level value chain metrics.

Step 3 (Analyze phase of E-DMAIC)
- Analyze satellite-level and 30,000-foot-level metrics looking for improvement opportunities.
- Analyze the enterprise as a whole looking for constraints, improvement opportunities, and new product opportunities, which could include acquisitions or selling portions of the business.

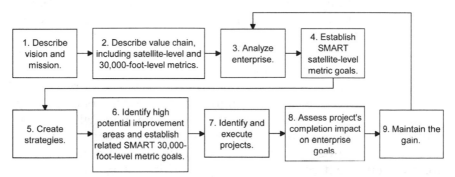

Figure 3.6: Aligning projects with business needs through E-DMAIC roadmap for project selection and P-DMAIC or DMADV roadmap for project execution.

Step 4 (Analyze phase of E-DMAIC)
  • Establish SMART goals that are consistent with the
    work from Step 3.
Step 5 (Analyze phase of E-DMAIC)
  • Create strategies from step analyses described in Step 3.
Step 6 (Analyze phase of E-DMAIC)
  • Identify high-potential areas and related 30,000-foot-
    level scorecard/dashboard metrics for focusing im-
    provement efforts using goals and the value-chain
    process map to help guide the selection process.
  • Establish 30,000-foot-level value chain metric goals
    with agree-to ownership and time for achievement. The
    project champion should be the owner of the metric
    that is to be improved.
  • Identify potential projects that are in alignment with
    determined business needs.
Step 7 (Improve phase of E-DMAIC)
  • Select and assign well-scoped projects that are not too
    large or too small.
  • Work for timely project completion of process using
    resource of champion and black belt or green belt with
    coaching.
Step 8 (Improve phase of E-DMAIC)
  • Assess project completion impact on enterprise goals.
Step 9 (Control phase of E-DMAIC)
  • Maintain the gains.
  • Repeat.

IEE 30,000-foot-level scorecard/dashboard metrics are high-
level operational or project metrics. The right metrics are needed
for the orchestration of the right activities. The E-DMAIC process
just described accomplishes this by linking improvement activities to business goals and to strategies that are aligned with these
goals through the use of analytics.

This strategy can also be used with other types of improvement
projects such as reliability excellence and behavior-based safety.
People in organizations often feel overwhelmed when facing
multiple improvement activities and when resources are in competition between associated projects. This system can tie all the
improvement practices together and prioritize the resources where
needed. It can help organizations understand and improve the
key drivers that affect the metrics and enterprise process scorecards.

3.2   IEE as a Business Strategy

In a work environment, tasks are completed. These tasks can lead to a response even though the procedures to perform them are not formally documented. Lead time is one potential response for the completion of a series of tasks. Another is the quality of the completed work. Reference will be made to important responses from a process as KPOVs, sometimes called the *Y*s of the process.

Sometimes the things that are completed within a work environment cause a problem to customers or create a great deal of waste; that is, overproduction, waiting, transportation, inventory, over-processing, motion, defects, and people utilization, which can be very expensive to an organization. Attempts to solve waste do not always address these problems from an overall system viewpoint. The organization might also have a variety of KPOVs, such as a critical dimension, overall lead time, a DPMO rate that could expose a hidden-factory rework issue currently not reported, customer satisfaction, and so on.

> When we manage simply toward goals and targets throughout the organization chart, we are managing to the Ys in the mathematical relationship $Y = f(X)$. This can lead to the wrong behavior; that is, the Enron effect. The way to make long-lasting improvements is through process changes or improving the management of the Xs.

For this type of situation, organizations often react to the up-and-down movements of the KPOV level over time in a firefighting mode, fixing the problems of the day. Frequent arbitrary tweaks to controllable process variables and noise (for example, material differences, operator-to-operator differences, machine-to-machine differences, and measurement imprecision) can cause excess variability and yield a large nonconforming proportion for the KPOV. Practitioners and management might think that their day-to-day problem-fixing activities are making improvements to the system. In reality, these activities often expend many resources without making any improvements to the process. Unless long-lasting process changes are made, the proportion of noncompliance will remain approximately the same.

When we manage simply toward goals and targets throughout the organization chart, we are managing to the *Y*s in the mathematical relationship $Y = f(X)$. This can lead to the wrong behavior;

that is, the Enron effect. The way to make long-lasting improvements is through process changes or improving the management of the *X*s that are shown in Figure 3.7.

Organizations that frequently encounter this type of situation have much to gain from the implementation of an IEE business strategy. They can better appreciate this potential gain when they consider all the direct and indirect costs associated with their current level of nonconformance.

The methodology described in this book is a deployment system that uses both statistical and nonstatistical tools. As Figure 3.1 illustrates, an E-DMAIC system can lead to an improvement project that follows the P-DMAIC roadmap. P-DMAIC is an enhanced version of the traditional Six Sigma DMAIC roadmap. The P-DMAIC roadmap offers additional component breakdown in the measure phase and true Lean tool integration.

In this business strategy, a practitioner applies the P-DMAIC roadmap either during a workshop or as a project after a workshop. The baseline for a created project would be determined through the metric-reporting process, as noted earlier, for the IEE scorecard/or dashboard as follows:

1. Assess process predictability.
2. When the process is considered predictable, formulate a prediction statement for the latest region of stability. The usual reporting format for this statement is the following:

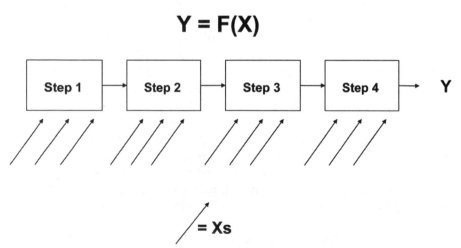

Figure 3.7: Magnitude of a process response as a function of its input levels.

(a)   When there is a specification requirement: nonconformance percentage or DPMO.

(b)   When there is no specification requirement: median response and 80 percent frequency of occurrence rate.

Figure 3.8 illustrates for continuous data the pull for project creation and benefit from the project as demonstrated in the 30,000-foot-level metric change. Figure 3.9 illustrates the same for an attribute response. It should be noted for continuous data that all individual values from the stable region of the process are used to create a voice of the process (VOP) distribution. The placements of specifications on this distribution provide an assessment of how well the process is performing relative to customer requirements, for example, a form of voice of the customer (VOC). While for attribute data, no distribution plot is needed since the centerline is a direct nonconformance rate estimate.

A resulting change process can have less waste and be more robust or indifferent to process noise variables. This effort can result in an improved process mean shift or reduced variability or both, which leads to quantifiable bottom-line monetary benefits.

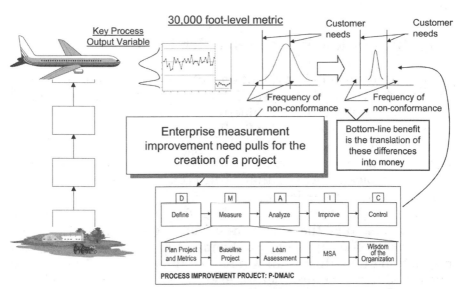

Figure 3.8: IEE Project creation, execution, and the benefits for a continuous response.

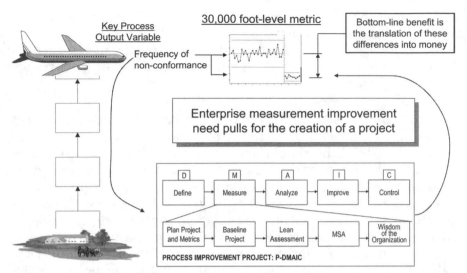

Figure 3.9: IEE Project creation, execution, and the benefits for an attribute response.

The success of IEE is a function of management commitment and an infrastructure that supports this commitment. However, this commitment does not need to come from the CEO level. This infrastructure can start anywhere. It can then spread throughout the company when system benefits materialize and can be shown to others.

3.3   Integration of Six Sigma with Lean

There has been much contention between Six Sigma and Lean functions. I will use the term *Lean* or *Lean thinking* to describe the application of Lean manufacturing, Lean production, or Lean enterprise-process principles to all processes. The Six Sigma community typically believes that Six Sigma comes first or is above Lean, relative to the application within an organization. Lean disciples typically believe that Lean comes first or is above Six Sigma, relative to application within an organization.

When people who have a strong foundation in Lean make the generalization that Lean improvement activities should be conducted before applying Six Sigma techniques, their thought process might be this: Lean will reduce the number of production lines producing the product. After this reduction, Six Sigma can be used to reduce variation. The reverse order may create redundant and unnecessary activities. For example, if three production lines are running, each with its own set of waste problems, it is far better to apply Lean initially to reduce the lines to one. From there, you can apply Six Sigma to reduce the variation.

> IEE integrates the two concepts, where the high-level metrics improvement need dictates which Lean or Six Sigma tools should be used at both the enterprise process and project execution level.

I do not believe that such a generalization should be made. In some situations, Lean methods should be considered first. There are other situations where Six Sigma methods should come first. In IEE there is no preset rule for which methodology precedes the other.

IEE integrates the two concepts, where the high-level metrics improvement need dictates which Lean or Six Sigma tools should be used at both the enterprise-process and project-execution level. For example, in the P-DMAIC project-execution roadmap, Lean tools are applied in both the measure and improve phases. When a Lean or Six Sigma methodology is used to achieve the project goal, the 30,000-foot-level metric change will be used to quantify statistically the change benefit on a continuing basis.

One reason why integration works so well is that the IEE approach does not require defining a project defect, as a traditional Six Sigma deployment does, where this definition would then impact the COPQ calculation. Not requiring a defect definition is very important since Lean metrics involve various waste measures, such as inventory or lead time, which do not have true specification criteria like manufactured components. COPQ calculations cannot really be made for these situations, since there are no true specifications; however, a CODND calculation can still be determined, where the objective of an IEE project is to reduce the CODND magnitude.

It is beneficial to dissolve any separately existing Six Sigma and Lean organizational functions. Organizations should strive to have the same person using an IEE methodology in which the most appropriate tool is applied for any given situation, whether the tool is Lean, Six Sigma, or combination of both.

3.4   Day-to-Day Business Management Using IEE

Organizations often experience much firefighting, where they react to the problems of the day. These organizations need a system, where they can replace many of their firefighting activities with fire prevention. This can be accomplished by cascading the measurement techniques described in this book.

With this strategy, metrics are orchestrated through a statistically based, high-level measurement system. Through the alignment of the satellite-level view with the 30,000-foot-level view and other high-level metrics, organizations can create meaningful scorecard/dashboard metrics that have a direct focus on the needs of the business at the operational level. The use of these metrics can improve the orchestration of day-to-day activities.

When we view our system using a set of cascading high-level individuals control chart that have infrequent subgrouping/sampling, behaviors can dramatically change for the better. Historically, metric systems often encouraged addressing individual day-to-day out-of-specification conditions as though they were special cause, even though they were truly common cause. This management style can lead to extensive firefighting. These fires, which often reappear after a temporary extinguishing, need immediate attention.

When there are common-cause variability problems resulting in a specification not being consistently met, the overall process needs to be changed to improve the metrics. Long-lasting improvements can be accomplished either through P-DMAIC projects, DFIEE/DFSS projects, or business-process-improvement events (BPIEs). P-DMAIC projects address the overall system's process steps and its metrics, including the measurement system itself and a control mechanism for the process that keeps it from returning to its previous unsatisfactory state. BPIEs are just-do-it improvement events that are needed by the system, but do not require the formalities of a P-DMAIC project.

With this approach, process-management teams might meet weekly to discuss their high-level 30,000-foot-level scorecard/dashboard operational metrics, while executives may review their metrics monthly. When an individuals control chart has infrequent subgrouping/sampling which shows a predictable process that does not yield a satisfactory level for the capability/performance metric, a project can be created. The P-DMAIC system experiences a pull for project creation by the need to improve the metrics.

This could become a green-belt project that is executed by a part-time process-improvement practitioner, who is within an organization's department function. The project might also become a large black-belt project that needs to address cross-functional issues. During project execution, both Six Sigma and Lean tools and methodologies need consideration to determine what needs to be done differently to achieve the desired enhanced-process response. Improvement direction might be generated quickly by executing a focused team-based kaizen event. In any case, when project improvements are made to the overall system, the 30,000-foot-level operational metric would change to an improved level.

Awareness of the 30,000-foot-level metrics and the results of project-improvement efforts should be made available to everyone, including those in the operations of the process. This information could be routinely posted using the visual-factory concept typically encountered in Lean implementations. Posting of information can improve the awareness and benefits of the system throughout the organization, which can lead to more buy in of the IEE methodology throughout the function. This can result in the stimulation of other improvement efforts that dramatically improve the overall satellite-level metrics.

This metric tracking and reporting approach along with the creation of improvement activities can alter management's focus, which might be on the problems of the day. It could lead to asking questions about the status of projects that would improve the overall operational process capability/performance metrics of the company. Behavioral changes would then start to take place that would focus on prevention rather reaction.

3.5   IEE and Innovation

Thurm (2007) states that:

> We've had management by objective and total quality management. Now it's time for the latest trend in business methodology: management by data. The success of enterprises as diverse as Harrah's Entertainment, Google, Capital One Financial and the Oakland A's has inspired case studies, books and consultants promising to help executives outpace rivals by collecting more information and analyzing it better.
>
> Google, the company that tracks every user keystroke on its Web site, also frees its engineers to spend 20% of their work time on self-directed projects. That has given birth to such programs as Google News, Gmail and, most significantly, AdSense for content, which places Google-brokered ads on other Web sites.

Dave Girouard, vice president and general manager of the Google unit building software for businesses, encourages his several hundred employees to use their self-directed time. "A lot of analytical stuff will give you incremental improvement, but it won't give you a big leap," he says. "You can't time or plan for innovation. It can't come from customer data. It has to come from the heart of somebody with an idea."

In addition, it is believed by some (*Business Week* 2007; Hindo 2007) that Lean Six Sigma inhibits rather than encourages innovation. This could be the case in an organization's Lean Six Sigma deployment, where focus is given to the search for projects and their completion. In these organizations, primary focus can be for

> Innovation with no framework for its creation and transition to a marketable product or service is not unlike an orchestra where every person uses his or her instrument to play individually composed musical selections at the same time.

black-belt or green-belt certification at project completion. With this deployment style, one can lose sight of the big picture.

In other cases, there can be a promulgation of this innovation-stifling belief by those who feel threatened. Some can be concern by the additional level of accountability and are looking for ways to undermine the deployment's implementation.

I have seen companies that were innovative; however, the organization did not benefit from the created technologies. This happens when either the technology did not fit into the company's product line or no system was in place to take the innovated product or service to market. Innovation with no framework for its creation and transition to a marketable product or service is not unlike an orchestra where every person uses their instrument to play individually composed musical selections at the same time. Individually, each musical presentation (innovated product or service) could sound very good, but the beauty of each musical piece is not heard or appreciated at the orchestra level (organization or company); that is the delivery of each musical selection did not have good overall orchestration.

The IEE system, which takes Lean Six Sigma and the balanced scorecard to the next level, enhances rather than detracts from innovation. By creating a system that captures VOC in the product-development cycle, greater emphasis can be given to using innovation to create products or services that are marketable. In this system, innovation is enabled by creating an infrastructure that breaks down creativity-usage barriers, which when orchestrated effectively can benefit the business as a whole.

The E-DMAIC system provides a framework for organizations to create a culture that is right for them relative to the amount of innovation nurturing and idea up-selling; that is, some companies by the nature of the business could need more out-of-the-box innovation thinking than other organizations.

For example, a company's created IEE infrastructure could include an annual get-together to stimulate or share thoughts about new product or service innovations. The overall company process to encourage innovation could include TRIZ (see List of Symbols and Acronyms) and other tools as part of existing ad hoc or innovation-generation practices that enhance the opportunity for creating innovative breakthrough-formulation opportunities.

Without the rigor of creating a system that embraces the orchestration of creativity and a go-to-market execution, chaos, the archenemy of innovation, can result.

3.6 Applying IEE

When we buy a product or service, we expect good service and delivery at the right price. If we take our car to the repair shop, we want the mechanic to work on the right problem with the right tool. At the enterprise level, a system is needed to assess how well processes are delivering per customer expectations. These expectations are typically captured in VOC studies and translated to process or product requirements. The scorecard/dashboard metrics that address how well these expectations are being met should follow a consistent methodology leading to the right activities. We want to create a system that encourages data investigation that formulates an understanding, which can be readily communicated to others. We want to create a system that becomes a means to achieving enterprise objectives. The techniques described in this chapter provide a system for addressing these needs.

IEE is much more than doing Six Sigma or Lean Six Sigma projects. IEE is a business measurement and improvement system that builds on the strengths of the project-driven Lean Six Sigma or Six Sigma methodologies and takes business scorecards/dashboards to the next level.

In traditional Six Sigma and Lean Six Sigma deployments, projects are usually selected from a steering committee list of potential projects. Created projects might sound financially worthwhile, but on completion these projects often do not truly deliver benefits to the overall enterprise. I have seen Six Sigma deployments stall when using this push for project creation approach. It is more desirable to have measurement improvement needs pull for project creation.

When organizations use satellite-level and 30,000-foot-level metrics for their scorecard/dashboard metrics, behaviors can dramatically change. In this system, when the measures degrade or indicate that an improvement is needed, a process owner initiates a corrective action that may result in a project. This would depend on whether the root-cause analysis revealed that the cause was common or special. The completion of these projects can result in fewer fires to fight and a long-term, sustainable process adjustment. With this approach, IEE is much more than doing Six Sigma or Lean Six Sigma projects. IEE is a business measurement and improvement system that builds on the strengths of the project-driven Lean Six Sigma or Six Sigma methodologies and takes business scorecard/dashboard to the next level. Figure 3.10 illustrates how the IEE infrastructure and metrics can create a long-lasting, data-driven culture.

The reader should also note how Figure 3.6 includes business analyses (step four) before strategy creation (step five). Often in hoshin kanri and other organizational deployments, the business jumps from Step 1 to Step 5. In reality, the executive team might have great insight and create the best possible strategy. However, this nine-step process formalizes the whole system so that the

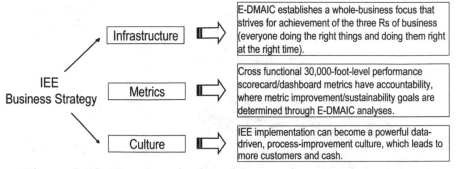

Figure 3.10: Creation of a data-driven and process-improvement culture through IEE.

strategy-development process is more repeatable. This will make the system less dependent on executive team intuition; that is, the company will become more data driven.

I have heard people complain that their company wastes resources and does things that do not make sense; however, their organization is not ready for the change. Organizations need to continually improve for survival. I hope this book provides the stimulus and direction needed for making enhancements to organizational scorecards, strategy building, and improvement systems.

4

Assessing Enterprise Goals and Strategic Alignment

Someone invites you to a seminar on trading stock options. You attend the session and the methodology sounds like a great investment opportunity. You decide to act so that you can increase the return on your investments. You decide to follow Deming's cycle of PDCA, as part of a hoshin kanri implementation. In the plan phase of the PDCA cycle, you attend training sessions, study training CDs, study software, and create your investment strategy. In the do phase you start investing. After a time you proceed to the check phase; however, your analysis indicates that things are not going well. You believe that you must be doing something wrong. The training sessions led you to believe things would be a lot better than you are experiencing. In the act phase you decide to attend more training sessions. Then you return to the plan phase of the PDCA cycle, make adjustments to your investment techniques, and proceed through the remaining steps of the cycle.

After going through the PDCA cycle several times, your assessment of your overall investment returns is not good. Then you decide to discuss the problems that you are having with other investors who took the training, hoping to learn something from them. In these discussions, you hear fantastic large-percentage trade-gain stories. You ask your colleagues more probing questions about how well they are doing overall. You are surprised when others provide an honest examination of their big-picture investment performance. You find that they are not doing any better than you are.

In the above-mentioned methodology, a plan was created from something that was thought to be beneficial, that is, options investing. No analyses were conducted to see if this was the best plan to achieve your overall desired objectives. Now consider what could have been done differently. Instead of starting with a plan, first define your vision, mission, and objectives. Then create performance metrics and conduct analyses that give insight to the best strategy to use.

Consider that the define phase finds that you want to have sufficient savings so that you don't have to worry about money in your retirement years. In the measure phase, a 30,000-foot-level scorecard/dashboard monthly tracking of rate of return for your financial holdings was not as good as you would have liked. A SMART (see Glossary) goal was set. In the analyze phase, you make assessments for determining the best *strategy* to accomplish your defined objectives. When conducting this analysis, keep in mind that you can't violate laws that govern the system. Determine the best approach that is not contrary to the laws of physics (see Glossary). For example, Isaac Newton's second law of motion is that force equals mass × acceleration ($F = MA$). Unless you are dealing with situations where Albert Einstein's theory of relativity applies, don't try to develop a strategy that is contrary to the proven $F = MA$ law. It is important to emphasize that out-of-the-box thinking is good for problem solving and strategic development. Care simply needs to be exercised when approaching current known physical law boundaries.

Statisticians know that the stock market motion is random and not predictable. Let's consider this a system law. Most options-trading models involve some form of prediction. Because of this assessment, we could conclude that options investing would not be a good strategy to pursue, since it competes against a system law.

In investing, as has been stated many times, the best way to obtain good capital growth is to make consistent, regular deposits to a balanced selection of equity funds that provide good returns. Let's consider this a proven system law. Investing in individual stocks is probably not a good idea for most investors because a stock-picking system would need to be developed. Mutual funds seem to be the best alternative; however, which one should we choose? Mutual fund brochures can be very deceiving.

This task initially seems to be overwhelming. Every financial magazine has a system and funds that are proclaimed to be the best. Brochures often relay one-year, five-year, and other time-interval return statements, which can be very deceiving. Results can depend on the start and stop date for each period. This form of reporting does not provide insight into what could have happened if a large investment had been made at some other point in time during the year, when a major market correction occurred immediately after the investment.

What we would like to assess is the output of various investment processes, mutual funds, a portfolio of various exchange-traded funds (ETFs), companies that manage portfolios, and the like. We could make this assessment using a spreadsheet where the growth of a hypothetical amount of money, say $10,000, was plotted monthly over a long time for the various investment options. We would look for a fund that provides not only long-haul consistent growth, but also has low month-to-month variability and small pullbacks during stock market correction periods. Since we are basically comparing investment processes, we can also make comparisons for arbitrarily chosen blocks of time that would contain major market corrections. Assuming that the funds were in existence at these times, we might compare funds during the periods 1982–1993, 1996–2003, 1999 to the present, and 1982 to the present.

> SMART goals should be consistent with the "laws of physics."

What we have just done is analyze data to gain insight to the best investment process or strategy for us, given our define-phase objectives. We can also assess whether our goals for the rate of return on investments are reasonable. SMART goals should be consistent with the system laws of physics. If they are not, an adjustment needs to be made or a completely different strategy needs to be investigated; perhaps investing in real estate.

The implementation of our strategy *at this point in time* is not inconsistent with the hoshin kanri Deming cycle of PDCA. We would start with the creation of a detailed plan for how much will be invested each month to reach our long-term objectives. The control phase of the E-DMAIC would assess the overall strategy over time to ensure that the mutual fund's performance did not degrade relative to market indexes and other competing funds.

This investment example is not much different from what happens in many companies. Are companies systematically performing analyses to choose their strategies, such as those in Tables 2.2, 2.3, and 2.4? Do companies, such as Enron, pick strategies that are not realistically possible?

Most employees don't get involved in creating strategic plans; they implement them. This book asks whether this is the best approach, and what is the current process for creating a strategic plan? One purpose of this chapter is to stimulate thought on this topic. In my opinion, most companies would agree that this is an area for improvement. E-DMAIC provides a systematic approach to address these opportunities (Breyfogle, 2008b).

Let's now consider the organizational metrics described in this chapter. Setting goals and reacting to individual points beyond these goals can lead to undesirable behaviors; for example, fire-fighting Deming's 94 percent common-cause issues as though they were special cause. Traditional scorecards encourage managers and decision makers to focus on targets at the expense of accepting measurement variability. Red–yellow–green scorecards can initially seem to be a good thing; however, this form of metric reporting can lead to a very large amount of wasted resources and playing games with the numbers.

The 30,000-foot-level metric is used in IEE to describe a high-level project or operation metric that has infrequent subgrouping/sampling so that short-term variations, which might be caused by typical variation in input levels, will result in charts that view these perturbations as common-cause issues. This objective, which is captured using 30,000-foot-level control charts, is different from traditional control chart objectives, which mean to identify special-cause conditions so that corrective actions can be taken (see Breyfogle, 2008c for chart-creation methods.). Examples of 30,000-foot-level metrics are lead time, inventory, defective rates, and a critical part dimension. There can be a

> The 30,000-foot-level metric is used in IEE to describe a high-level project or operation metric that has infrequent subgrouping/sampling so that short-term variations, which might be caused by typical variation in input levels, will result in charts that view these perturbations as common-cause issues. This objective, which is captured using 30,000-foot-level control charts, is different from traditional control-chart objectives, which mean to identify special-cause conditions so that corrective actions can be taken.

drill-down to a 20,000-foot-level metric if there is an alignment, such as the largest product defect type.

The purpose of the 30,000-foot-level chart is to view a process response from a high-level airplane view to determine whether a process is predictable or has common-cause variability. If the process output from common-cause variability is not satisfactory or what we desire, then a process-improvement effort would experience a pull for project creation. This is in contrast to traditional control charts, which are created for timely identification when special causes occur so that adjustments can be made to bring the process back in control. As a business metric, 30,000-foot-level reporting can lead to more efficient resource utilization and less manipulation of the numbers.

> The purpose of the 30,000-foot-level chart is to view a process response from a high-level, airplane view to determine whether a process is predictable; that is, has common cause variability. If the process output from common cause variability is not satisfactory or what we desire, then a process improvement project would be pulled for creation.

Spear and Bowen (1999) articulated four Lean "DNA" rules and their view of the Toyota reasoning process. Jackson (2006) added a fifth rule with some rewording of the original rules. To expand the DNA definition to an IEE system, I added four additional rules with some rewording of previous rules. The IEE DNA rules are:

Rule 1. *Standardize processes and work:* Create efficient and effective processes that have reduced variability and improved quality.

Rule 2. *Zero ambiguity:* Internal and external customer requirements are perfectly clear.

Rule 3. *Flow the process:* Material and information flow directly with minimal waste and variation.

Rule 4. *Speak with data:* Compile and present the most appropriate data so that the right question is answered, and both statistical and visualization tools are used effectively.

Rule 5. *Develop leaders who are teachers:* Leaders need to truly understand and then coach employees in E-DMAIC and P-DMAIC execution.

Rule 6. *Align work to the value chain:* Align and document the processes in the value chain so that information is readily accessible to fulfill employee and supplier needs.

Rule 7. *Report metrics at the 30,000-foot-level:* avoid scorecard systems that track against goals or calendar point performance metric reporting, which often leads to wasted resources through firefighting. Metrics need to be created so that there are no games played with the numbers.

Rule 8. *Build strategies after analyzing the value chain, its metrics, and goals:* avoid creating strategies in isolation and aligning work activities to these strategies. Execution possibilities for strategy statements, such as those in Section 3.4, are very team dependent and can lead to detrimental activities for the enterprise as a whole.

Rule 9. *Let metric improvement needs pull for project creation:* a push for a project-creation system can lead to the suboptimization of processes that don't favorably impact the business as a whole.

The application of the system described in this book can become the enabling means to receive both the Malcolm Baldrige Award and the Shingo Prize (see Glossary).

4.1 Do You Have a Strategy?

In the article "Are you sure you have a strategy?" Donald Hambrick and James Fredrickson (2001) describe shortcomings with developed frameworks for strategic analysis. They point out that what is missing is guidance for what constitutes a strategy and what should be the outcome. This chapter blends article highlights within E-DMAIC.

> What is missing is guidance for what constitutes a strategy and what should be the outcome.

"Strategy has become a catchall term used to mean whatever one wants it to mean. Executives now talk about their 'service strategy,' their 'branding strategy,' their 'acquisition strategy,' or whatever kind of strategy that is on their mind at any given moment. But strategists – whether they are CEOs of established firms, division presidents, or entrepreneurs – must have a strategy, an integrated, overarching concept of how the business will achieve its objectives."

Consider these statements of strategy drawn from actual documents and announcements of several companies:

"Our strategy is to be the low-cost provider."

"We're pursuing a global strategy."

"The company's strategy is to integrate a set of regional acquisitions."

"Our strategy is to provide unrivaled customer service."

"Our strategic intent is to always be the first mover."

"Our strategy is to move from defense to industrial applications."

"What do these declarations have in common? Only that none of them is a strategy. They are strategic threads, mere elements of strategy. But they are no more strategies than Dell Computer's strategy can be summed up as selling direct to customers or than Hannibal's strategy was to use elephants to cross the Alps; and their use reflects an increasingly common syndrome,– the catchall fragmentation of strategy" (Hambrick and Fredrickson, 2001). These described strategic elements are not inconsistent with the strategy in Figure 2.4, in which a corporation stated on its web page.

"Executives then communicate these strategic threads to their organizations in the mistaken belief that doing so will help managers make tough choices. But how does knowing that their firm is pursuing an 'acquisition strategy' or a 'first-mover strategy' help the vast majority of managers do their job or set priorities?" (Hambrick and Fredrickson, 2001).

Business leaders must have a strategy to meet their objectives. Without a strategy, time and resources can be wasted on piecemeal, disparate activities. Without a strategy, mid-level managers will fill the void with their interpretation of what the business should be doing, typically resulting in a disjointed set of activities.

The define phase of E-DMAIC includes the company's vision, mission, values, and Jim Collins' three circles: What can you do to be the best in the world? What drives your economic engine? What are you deeply passionate about? (Collins, 2001). The organization's value chain along with satellite-level and 30,000-foot-level scorecard/dashboard metrics are created in the measure phase of E-DMAIC.

With IEE, organizations are now in a position to assess the current state of the high-level value-chain metrics to determine the most appropriate goals for an organization. These goals blended with a strategic analysis can then provide inputs to a strategy, which is a centrally integrated, externally oriented concept on what tactics can be created to achieve the desired results.

4.2   Enterprise Process Goal Setting

Vince Lombardi changed the National Football League (NFL) Green Bay Packers, who were perpetually losing at the time, into an NFL dynasty. Coach Lombardi said, "If you are not keeping score, you are just practicing."

Dr. Deming (1986) states, "If you have a stable system, then there is no use to specify a goal. You will get whatever the system will deliver. A goal beyond the capability of the system will not be reached.... If you do not have a stable system, then there is again no point in setting a goal. There is no way to know what the system will produce: it has no capability."

Dr. Lloyd S. Nelson (Deming, 1986) stated, "If you can improve productivity, or sales, or quality, or anything else, by 5 percent next year without a rational plan for improvement, then why were you not doing it last year?"

> The implication of Deming's statement is that simple goal setting alone will not yield an improved output. For an improved output, organizations need to give due diligence to bettering the process.

When organizations establish scorecard goals, much care needs to be exercised. Goals should be SMART. However, these guidelines are often violated. Arbitrary goals set for individuals or organizations can be very counterproductive and costly.

The implication of Deming's statement is that simple goal setting alone will not yield an improved output. For an improved output, organizations need to give due diligence to bettering the process. This book focuses on the creation of more customers and cash (MC^2), not the simple creation of arbitrary goals throughout the organization, which can lead to the wrong activities or strategies that often lead to interpretation and action-item inconsistencies.

In E-DMAIC, satellite-level and 30,000-foot-level scorecard/dashboard metrics are examined over time before financial goals are established. The assessment of these noncalendar bounded metrics helps with the creation of SMART goals. This assessment could lead to the following mean monthly satellite-level metric goals:

- *Sales growth:* 10 percent
- *Operating margins:* 20 percent
- *ROCE (return on capital employed):* 20 percent

Other organizational goals that could be tracked at the 30,000-foot-level scorecard/dashboard metric level are the following:

- *Environmental:* Energy cost reductions of at least 25 percent over 3 years
- *New products:* 30 percent of products sold have been available 5 years or less

Satellite-level enterprise process goals can be drilled down to 30,000-foot-level goals and then to specific projects that facilitate the process of achieving these goals (see Breyfogle, 2008b).

4.3   Strategic Analyses

Strategic thinking is important to the business. A strategic analysis includes (Hambrick and Fredrickson, 2001) the following:

- Industrial analysis
- Customer or marketplace trends
- Environmental forecast
- Competitor analysis
- Assessment of internal strengths, weakness, resources

Organizations often build strategies around statements such as "develop strategic relationship with industry leaders." How does an organization interpret and measure success against a statement like this? What makes matters worse is that these strategies are then cascaded throughout the whole organization and functional goals are set against them. Could there be different interpretations for these strategies? Of course there could. What happens when leadership changes? Do the strategies change? I would again say yes, and the change could lead to havoc with a redo of many organizational metrics.

The E-DMAIC system described later overcomes these issues.

4.4   Strategy Development

A strategy needs to be dynamic so that it can address timely changes and flexible so that it can address multiple options. It needs to be able to form an effective assessment of current conditions for the creation of a meaningful 2 to 3-year plan. Most strategic plans emphasize only one or two components of what is truly needed.

Figure 4.1 describes a process that organizations can walk through to execute the five critical elements for strategy development (Hambrick and Fredrickson, 2001). These five elements, requiring choice, preparation, and investment, also need alignment within the developed strategy.

Criteria for testing the quality of a strategy (Hambrick and Fredrickson, 2001) are the following:

1. *Does your strategy fit with what's going on in the environment?*

   Is there healthy profit potential where you're headed? Does your strategy align with the key success factors of your chosen environment?

2. *Does your strategy exploit your key resources?*

   With your particular mix of resources, does this strategy give you a good head start on competitors? Can you pursue this strategy more economically than your competitors?

3. *Will your envisioned differentiators be sustainable?*

   Will competitors have difficulty matching you? If not, does your strategy explicitly include a ceaseless regimen of innovation and opportunity creation?

4. *Are the elements of your strategy internally consistent?*

   Have you made choices of areas, vehicles, differentiators, staging, and economic logic? Do they all fit and mutually reinforce each other?

5. *Do you have enough resources to pursue this strategy?*

   Do you have the money, managerial time and talent, and other capabilities to do all you envision? Are you sure that you're not spreading your resources too thin, only to be left with a collection of feeble positions?

6. *Can your strategy be implemented?*

   Will your key constituencies allow you to pursue this strategy? Can your organization make it through the transition? Are you and your management team able and willing to lead the required changes?

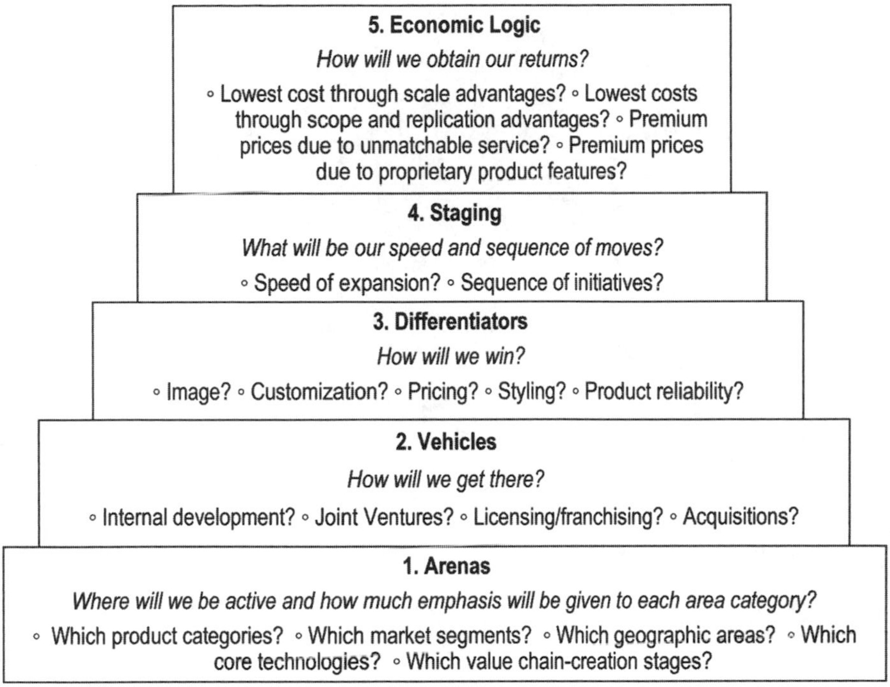

5. Economic Logic

How will we obtain our returns?

∘ Lowest cost through scale advantages? ∘ Lowest costs through scope and replication advantages? ∘ Premium prices due to unmatchable service? ∘ Premium prices due to proprietary product features?

4. Staging

What will be our speed and sequence of moves?

∘ Speed of expansion? ∘ Sequence of initiatives?

3. Differentiators

How will we win?

∘ Image? ∘ Customization? ∘ Pricing? ∘ Styling? ∘ Product reliability?

2. Vehicles

How will we get there?

∘ Internal development? ∘ Joint Ventures? ∘ Licensing/franchising? ∘ Acquisitions?

1. Arenas

Where will we be active and how much emphasis will be given to each area category?

∘ Which product categories? ∘ Which market segments? ∘ Which geographic areas? ∘ Which core technologies? ∘ Which value chain-creation stages?

Figure 4.1: Five strategic development elements.

Creating a vision begins with an understanding of the current situation. An organization needs to understand the hundreds of controllable and uncontrollable forces that pull them in multiple directions so that they can make appropriate adjustments. The organization's success depends upon how well they accomplish these. Some basic *today* and *in the future* strategic planning questions are (Hamel and Prahalad, 1994):

- Describe customers that you serve? (today and the future)
- What channels are used to reach your customers? (today and the future)
- Describe your competitors? (today and the future)
- Describe your competitive advantage basis? (today and the future)
- Describe the source for your margins? (today and the future)
- What are your unique skills or capabilities? (today and the future).

5

Firefighting Reduction through IEE

Much time and resources can be spent redirecting people's efforts to working on the crisis of the day. This practice takes people away from planned work, often causing delays, which could lead to the next fire. You may not be able to relate to this, but top leadership could have been promoted over the years because of their firefighting skills.

5.1   Metrics and the Problem of the Day

Organizational metrics and goal setting can get really crazy. One plant had safety banners express mailed to their location for posting since a goal was not being met. This plant had been telling headquarters that they were making improvements, but suddenly things got worse. A later examination of the organization's safety data using our Integrated Enterprise Excellence (IEE) scorecard system indicated that no improvements were being made. Their red–yellow–green scorecard improvement approach was not fixing anything.

It is interesting that organizations even have conference rooms that they call war rooms, where the same problems are fought over and over daily or weekly. Good firefighters can get an adrenalin rush from the quick priority changes and the need for immediate action. The best firefighters can be highly rewarded. The fire-prevention team never seems to be recognized equally by management. This war room strategy drains the organization of its resources and causes companies to lose focus.

The IEE system helps organizations create a measurement and improvement system that gets them out of the firefighting mode and into the fire-prevention mode. Let's continue examining traditional metric reporting with the intent of evolving to a system that gets organizations out of the firefighting mode.

5.2   Example 5.1: Culture Firefighting or Fire Prevention?

In this example, a traditional approach will be used initially to address nonconformance issues. A high-level IEE alternative approach will then be presented, along with its benefits. Breyfogle (2008c) describes for continuous and attribute data the mechanics of creating this alternative metric reporting format.

An organization collects data and reacts whenever an out-of-specification condition occurs or a goal is not met. The following example dialog is what could happen when attempts are made to fix all out-of-specification problems whenever they occur in a manufacturing or service environment. This scenario could apply equally to a business service process whenever the goals of an organization are not being met.

Consider a product that has specification limits of 72–78. An organization might react to collected data in the following manner:

- First datum: 76.2
  - Everything is OK.
- Second datum: 78.2
  - Joe, go fix the problem.
- Data: 74.1, 74.1, 75.0, 74.5, 75.0, 75.0
  - Everything OK; Joe must have done a good job!
- Next datum: 71.8
  - Mary, fix the problem.
- Data: 76.7, 77.8, 77.1, 75.9, 76.3, 75.9, 77.5, 77.0, 77.6, 77.1, 75.2, 76.9
  - Everything OK; Mary must have done a good job!

- Next datum: 78.3
  - Harry, fix the problem.
- Next data: 72.7, 76.3
  - Everything OK; Harry must have fixed the problem.
- Next datum: 78.5
  - Harry, seems like there still is a problem.
- Next data: 76.0, 76.8, 73.2
  - Everything OK; the problem must be fixed now.
- Next datum: 78.8
  - Sue, please fix the problem that Harry could not fix.
- Next data: 77.6, 75.2, 76.8, 73.8, 75.6, 77.7, 76.9, 76.2, 75.1, 76.6, 76.6, 75.1, 75.4, 73.0, 74.6, 76.1
  - Everything is great; give Sue an award!
- Next datum: 79.3
  - Get Sue out there again. She is the only one who knows how to fix the problem.
- Next data: 75.9, 75.7, 77.9, 78
  - Everything is great again!

A plot of this information is shown in Figure 5.1. From this plot, we see that the previously described reaction to the out-of-specification conditions individually did not improve the

Reaction to the out-of-specification conditions individually did not improve the process or prevent the likelihood of having problems in the future. The firefighters did not fix anything.

process or prevent the likelihood of having problems in the future. The firefighters did not fix anything.

Figure 5.2 shows a re-plot of the data as an individuals control chart. The control limits in this figure are calculated from the data. Specifications in no way affect the control limits. This chart is a statement of the Voice Of the Process (VOP) relative to whether the process is considered in statistical control or not, stable or not. Since people often have difficulty in understanding what *in control* means, I prefer to use the term *predictable*.

These lower and upper control limits (LCL and UCL, respectively) represent a ±3 sampling standard deviation around the mean ($\bar{x}$). For this type of chart, the ±3 sampling standard deviation is usually considered to be 2.66 times the mean of the adjacent-time-value moving range (see Breyfogle 2008c). Since the up-and-down

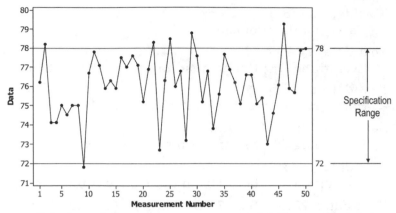

Figure 5.1: Reacting to common-cause variability as though it were special cause.

movements are within the UCL and LCL and there are no unusual patterns, we would conclude that there are no special-cause data conditions and that the source of process variability is a common cause. The process is predictable.

Some readers might think that the control limits seem to be too wide and wonder about tightening up the control limits. My response to that is this:

> The control limits are considered the VOP and are directly calcu-lated from the data. In some cases the control limits could be too wide. This occurrence is typically a function of data-collection pro-cedures or a special-cause condition. When this occurs, you would work these issues instead of changing the control limits. For this data set, this is not the case.
>
> Most think action limits (i.e., VOC), when they decide to tighten control limits. This may seem to be a good thing, but is *not*. If you tighten the control limits to be narrower than the VOP, the result is most certainly an increase in firefighting.

This organization had been reacting to the out-of-specification conditions as though they were special cause. The focus on fixing out-of-specification conditions often leads to firefighting. When fire-fighting activities involve tweaking the process, additional variability can be introduced, degrading the process rather than improving it.

Deming noted the following:

- "A fault in the interpretation of observations, seen everywhere, is to suppose that every event (defect, mistake, accident) is attributable to someone (usually the nearest at hand), or is related to some special event."

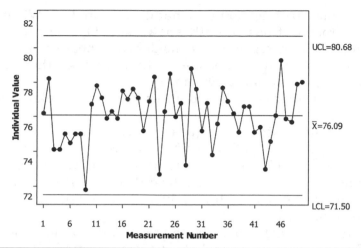

No.	Data	MR	No.	Data	MR	No.	Data	MR	No.	Data	MR	No.	Data	MR
1	76.20		11	77.80	1.10	21	76.90	1.70	31	75.20	2.40	41	75.10	1.50
2	78.20	2.00	12	77.10	0.70	22	78.30	1.40	32	76.80	1.60	42	75.40	0.30
3	74.10	4.10	13	75.90	1.20	23	72.70	5.60	33	73.80	3.00	43	73.00	2.40
4	74.10	0.00	14	76.30	0.40	24	76.30	3.60	34	75.60	1.80	44	74.60	1.60
5	75.00	0.90	15	75.90	0.40	25	78.50	2.20	35	77.70	2.10	45	76.10	1.50
6	74.50	0.50	16	77.50	1.60	26	76.00	2.50	36	76.90	0.80	46	79.30	3.20
7	75.00	0.50	17	77.00	0.50	27	76.80	0.80	37	76.20	0.70	47	75.90	3.40
8	75.00	0.00	18	77.60	0.60	28	73.20	3.60	38	75.10	1.10	48	75.70	0.20
9	71.80	3.20	19	77.10	0.50	29	78.80	5.60	39	76.60	1.50	49	77.90	2.20
10	76.70	4.90	20	75.20	1.90	30	77.60	1.20	40	76.60	0.00	50	78.00	0.10

	Data	MR
Mean =	76.09	1.73
UCL =	76.09 + 2.66(1.73) =	80.68
LCL =	76.09 - 2.66(1.73) =	71.50

Figure 5.2: Control chart illustration of common-cause variability.

- "We shall speak of faults of the system as common causes of trouble, and faults from fleeting events as special causes."
- "Confusion between common causes and special causes leads to frustration of everyone, and leads to greater variability and to higher costs, exactly contrary to what is needed."
- "I should estimate that in my experience most troubles and most possibilities for improvement add up to proportions something like this: 94 percent belong to the system (responsibility of management), 6 percent [are] special."

Let's revisit the data using a Deming approach. When data are in statistical control, we can say that the process is predictable.

The next obvious question is: What do you predict? When a process control chart has recently shown stability, we can lump all data in this stable region and consider that these data are a random sample of the future, assuming that nothing either positively or negatively changes the system.

Using this approach, we could create the dot plot shown in Figure 5.3.

An attribute assessment (pass or fail) for this data would yield a 12 percent (6/50) defective rate. However, some of these failures or nonfailures are borderline and, if we rerun this experiment, we could get a significantly different response. Also, the overall response distribution has no impact on our statement relative to nonconformance.

A better approach would be to create a probability plot of the data from this stable control chart region. Figure 5.4 shows the results, where a probability plot is an estimated cumulative percent-less-than distribution plot. For example, a best estimate for this population is that about 0.629 percent will be below 72 and 87.768 percent will be less than 78. (See Breyfogle 2008c for creating and interpreting probability plots.)

From this analysis, we conclude that the process has an approximate 13 percent common-cause, nonconformance rate both now and in the future, unless something either negatively or positively impacts the *overall* process. If the financial impact of this nonconformance rate is unsatisfactory, this measurement could pull for the creation of a project to improve the process.

Note, 13 percent is determined from the probability plot through the following calculations:

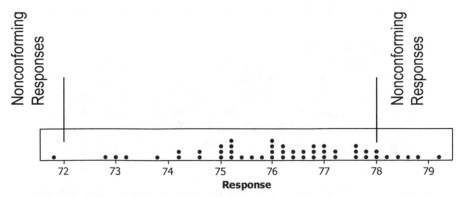

Figure 5.3: Dot plot attribute estimation of process percentage nonconformance rate.

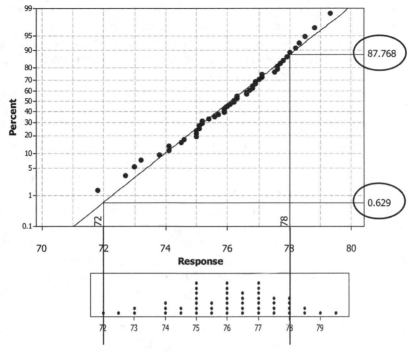

Figure 5.4: Probability plot of a continuous process output response from a stable process, with nonconformance rate estimation.

- 0.629 + (100 – 87.768) = 12.861, rounded to 13 percent
  - 0.629 is the estimated percentile below the specification limit
  - (100 – 87.768) is the estimated percentile above the specification limit

Inconsistent and ineffective organizational metric reporting can lead to much waste. The methodology described above is a consistent process, which can lead to fewer firefighting activities:

Reiterating, IEE scorecard/dashboard metrics reporting process is the following:

1. Assess process predictability.
2. When the process is considered predictable, formulate a prediction statement for the latest region of stability. The usual reporting format for this statement is the following:
   a. When there is a specification requirement: nonconformance percentage or defects per million opportunities (DPMO).
   b. When there is no specification requirement: median response and 80 percent frequency of occurrence rate.

The described satellite-level and 30,000-foot-level control charts and process capability/performance metric statements can be created for a variety of situations. A process capability/performance metric statement can quantify the magnitude of disconnection between VOP and VOC.

It is important to note that this described prediction analysis applies to stable processes. In the stable region of processes, data need to be analyzed collectively for the purpose of gaining insight to improvement opportunities. This is in contrast to attempting to explain why one datum point is up and another point is down.

For nonpredictable processes, understanding is gained through data examination. For example, a process change could have resulted in the shift in the process response to a new region of stability. For this situation, each region of stability needs to be examined separately. Another example is when distinct multiple distributions are prevalent; for example, the holiday season needs to be examined separately from the rest of the year. The final example is when one point occurs beyond the control limits. For this situation, it could be appropriate to assess one occurrence as an individual special-cause condition while collectively analyzing all the other points from the region of stability.

6

Understanding Nonconformance

Nonconformance is deviation from a product or transaction requirement or standard. Nonconformance can also be described as a discrepancy, error, fault, problem, or anomaly. Corrective action is considered to be a general procedure description for the correction and control of nonconformities. This chapter discusses the question of how to efficiently and effectively examine data and address corrective actions.

The example in the previous chapter showed a voice of the customer (VOC) output requirement response of 72–78. If a product were to be outside these specifications, the incident would be considered noncompliant. What we want to examine is how an organization's culture responds relative to addressing nonconformance. Organizational attempts to solve all noncompliant transactions from a process can lead to a large amount of firefighting.

Organizational cultures that embrace this philosophy could be working hard to use inspection to put quality into the product or service. It can take a large amount of resources to support this type of culture. What we would like to create is a measurement and improvement system so that we are not expending so much effort fixing common-cause issues as though they were special cause. We would like to create a culture that systematically reduces the likelihood of common-cause process-variability issues, so that there is a reduction in the frequency of similar problems occurring in the future.

Many times we consider that all nonconformance instances in a process are equal. But is this statement true? Consider the following:

> You are traveling by airplane, and the flight departs late in the day and has a short connection-time stop. If the airline on-time flight-departure statistics consider a flight that departs no more than 15 minutes late as an on-time departure (i.e., 15 minutes late is a specification), then a flight that is 14 minutes late is considered to be on time and a flight that is 16 minutes late is considered to be not on time, or a noncompliance incident.
>
> As an airline customer would you be equally dissatisfied with a 16-minute-late departure as a 2-hour-late departure? In the airline statistics, both late flights count equally as a nonconformance. However, with a 16-minute-late departure you would probably be able to make your connection, while a 2-hour-late departure could mean that you would have to spend the night in your connecting flight's city.

For this situation, I would suspect that you would be more dissatisfied with the 2-hour-late departure than the 16-minute-late departure. Pass or fail data analysis relative to the 15-minute-late-departure criterion to determine percentage nonconformance would be an attribute response assessment.

As an alternative to this attribute data analysis approach, a sample of the continuous data could be used to determine whether the process is predictable. If it is, the distribution of the continuous response data from the stable region on the individual's control chart could be used to create an estimate of the percentage of flights expected to be later than 15 minutes. For this continuous data analysis, we need to collect more details about flight departure times, for example, flights that departed 3.5 or 32 minutes late, and flights that departed –3 minutes late (i.e., 3 minutes early). However, in general, a continuous response assessment would provide a better prediction estimate than an attribute response assessment. In addition, we can gain a lot more insight with a continuous response analysis. For example, from a continuous response analysis we could also estimate the percentage of flights that would be 30 minutes late.

When creating an organization's data-driven culture, we need to be conscious of how we collect and examine data so that we get the most information possible from our analyses.

6.1 Creating an Enhanced Results-Achieving Culture through Wisely Selected Performance Metrics

People often talk about wanting to make organizational cultural change. An inordinate amount of money can be spent on workshops and consultations addressing cultural change issues, often with questionable results.

Consider an organization that wants to create a more data-driven, decision-making culture. Examining and reacting to these data differently can be the impetus for making a real long-lasting culture enhancement. In the last chapter's example, the organization reacted to every nonconformance issue as though it were a special cause. This situation is not much different from organizations that use war rooms to identify the problems of the day or week, so that people can be deployed to firefight the latest issues. In the previous example, Sue received an award for a long string of conforming production, and Harry was reprimanded for not having a long string of conforming production after his production work. In reality, these data were randomly generated. Sue was simply lucky, while Harry was unlucky. The organization culture was attacking common-cause issues as though they were special cause.

Many resources can be wasted when an organizational culture takes on corrective actions for every out-of-specification condition or individual occurrence beyond goals as though these are special-cause occurrences. Attempting to identify why individual points are beyond a specification or goal is not an effective structured root-cause-analysis approach that leads to long-lasting preventive actions, which reduce the likelihood of future occurrence of a similar problem.

Consider how our organizational behavior would change were we to say that we have a predictable process where we expect

> Consider how our organizational behavior would change were we to say that we have a predictable process where we expect to have about 13 percent nonconformance, unless we do something different to the underlying process.

to have about 13 percent nonconformance, unless we do something different to the underlying process. In this project-creation pull system, we would then follow the systematic IEE project-execution roadmap for timely resolution. In this new culture, we would focus on identifying and improving or controlling the Xs that impact the Ys.

When there is a report out of a 30,000-foot-level scorecard/dashboard chart showing a need for improvement, management would be asking for project status since they understand that most recent up-and-down movements are from common-cause variability. When projects are not on schedule, management would be asking for explanations and what could be done to get back on schedule and expedite the project's completion.

Both public and private organizations frequently look at human and machine performance data similar to the situation just described and then make judgments based on the data. Production supervisors might constantly review production output by employee, by machine, by work shift, by day of the week, by product line, and so forth. In the service sector, an administrative assistant's output of letters and memos may be monitored daily. In call centers around the world, the average time spent per call could be monitored and used to counsel low-performing employees. The efficiency of computer programmers could be monitored through the tracking of lines of code produced per day. In the legal department, the number of patents secured on the company's behalf could be assessed over time. Whenever an organization reacts to individual excursions beyond requirements and specifications without examining the system as a whole, it could be reacting to common-cause situations as though they were special cause.

To illustrate this point further I will use the example of an organization that monitored the frequency of safety memos. A safety memo is written indicating that the number of accidents involving injuries during the month of July was 16, up by 2 from 14 such injuries a year ago in July. The memo declares this increase in accidents to be unacceptable and requires all employees to watch a mandatory, 30-minute safety video by the end of August. At an average wage rate of $10 per hour, the company payroll of 1500 employees affected the August bottom line by $7500 plus wasted time getting to and from the conference room. This does not even consider the time spent issuing memos reminding people to attend, reviewing attendance rosters looking for laggards, and so forth.

I am not saying that safety and productivity are not important to an organization. I am saying, as did Deming, that perhaps 94 percent of the output of a person or machine is a result of the system that management has put in place for use by the workers. If performance is poor, 94 percent of the time it is the system that must be modified for improvements to occur. Only 6 percent of the time is problem due to special causes. Knowing the difference between special-cause and common-cause variations can affect how organizations react to data and the success they achieve using the methods of a Six Sigma strategy. For someone to reduce the frequency of safety accidents from common cause, an organization would need to look at its systems collectively over a long period to determine what should be done to processes that lead to safety problems. Reacting to an individual month that does not meet a criterion can be both counterproductive and very expensive.

One simple question that should be repeated time and time again as IEE implementation proceeds is this: Is the variation I am observing common cause or special cause? The answer to this simple question has a tremendous impact on the action managers and workers take in response to process and product information. And those actions have a tremendous impact on worker motivation and worker self-esteem.

> Common-cause variability of the process could or might not cause a problem relative to meeting customer needs. We don't know the results until we collectively compare the process output relative to a specification or requirement.

Common-cause variability of the process could or might not cause a problem relative to meeting customer needs. We don't know the results until we collectively compare the process output relative to a specification or requirement. This is much different from reacting to individual points that do not meet specification limits. When we treat common-cause data collectively, we focus on what should be done to improve the process. When reacting to an individual event that is beyond specification limits where only common-cause events are occurring, we focus on this individual point as though it were a special-cause condition, rather than on the process information collectively. This type of investigation wastes resources and can lead to process changes that actually degrade future system performance. It is important to note that special causes usually receive more attention because of high visibility. However, more gains can often be made by continually working on common cause.

Reiterating, variations of common cause resulting in out-of-specification conditions do not mean that one cannot or should not do anything about it. What it does mean is that you need to focus on improving the process, not just firefight individual situations that happen to be out of specification. However, it is first essential to identify whether the condition is common cause or special cause. If the condition is common cause, data are used collectively when comparisons are made relative to the frequency of how the process will perform relative to specification needs. If an individual point or points are determined to be special cause from a process point of view, we then need to address what was different about them.

One of the most effective quality tools for distinguishing between common-cause and special-cause variations is the simple-to-learn and easy-to-use control chart. The problem with control charts is that they are so simple that many managers and workers misunderstand and misuse them to the detriment of product and process quality. In Chapter 7, I will elaborate on the satellite-level and 30,000-foot-level control charting procedures, which can greatly enhance an organization's success. This scorecard/dashboard format can reduce the frustration and expense associated with firefighting activities within an organization.

6.2   Example 6.1: Red–Yellow–Green Graphical Reporting Alternative

Figure 2.9 presented a red–yellow–green dashboard graphic report out for this attribute situation; that is, a shipment was either on time or not. The following observations were made from the chart, where there were seven yellow and six red occurrences:

Month	Jan-03	Feb-03	Mar-03	Apr-03	May-03	Jun-03	Jul-03	Aug-03	Sep-03	Oct-03	Nov-03	Dec-03	Jan-04
Percent Late Deliveries	0.38	3.16	3.59	1.44	2.86	3.23	0.88	3.20	1.64	0.74	2.11	1.52	2.45
Yellow if equal to or higher than	0	0	0	0	0	0	0	0	0	0	0	0	0
Red if equal to or higher than	2.2	2.2	2.2	2.2	2.2	2.2	2.2	2.2	2.2	2.2	2.2	2.2	2.2

Reiterating, the IEE analysis process that will be followed below, the IEE scorecard/dashboard metric reporting process uses the following procedure:

1. Assess process predictability.
2. When the process is considered predictable, formulate a prediction statement for the latest region of stability. The usual reporting format for this statement is as follows:
   a. When there is a specification requirement: nonconformance percentage or DPMO.

b. When there is no specification requirement: median response and 80 percent frequency of occurrence rate.

Applying the IEE scorecard/dashboard metric reporting process to this data set yields the following: (see Figure 6.1)

1. When there are no occurrences beyond the two horizontal lines (i.e., upper and lower control limits), no patterns, or data shifts, the process is said to be in control. When this occurs, we have no reason to not believe that the up-and-down monthly variability is the result of common-cause variability; the

Traditional Performance Reporting Example – Red-Yellow-Green Scorecard

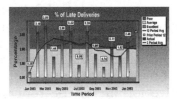

IEE Improved Reporting for Process Assessment and Improvement

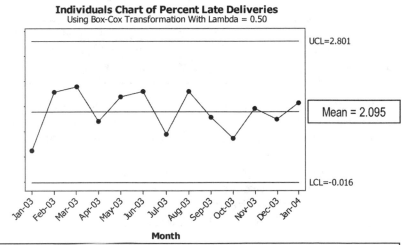

Predictable process with an approximate 2.1% non-conformance rate

(i.e., Using the current process, deliveries will be late about 2% of the time.)

Figure 6.1: Illustration of IEE improved attribute pass/fail process output response reporting: Red–yellow–green (see Figure 2.9) versus IEE Reporting.

process can be described as predictable. As previously noted, the purpose of red–yellow–green charting is to stimulate improvements. The control chart in Figure 6.1 provides an IEE assessment of how well this is accomplished; that is, it appears that no improvements were made (see Breyfogle (2008c) for chart-creation methods)

2. The next question to address is what prediction statement can be made. Since the process is predictable, we can consider the past data from the region of stability to be a random sample of the future. Unless a fundamental process improvement is made, we can expect our attribute response process output of late deliveries to be approximately 2.1 percent, or the centerline of the control chart. An IEE statement about this process is that it is predictable with an approximate nonconformance rate of 2.1 percent.

The figure includes an alternative format statement similar to what you might hear in a news report. I prefer a consistent reporting format that makes a statement about predictability and then what is predicted; however, including this alternative format in the report out can improve communications of the concepts. I will include this form of reporting for other volume report outs.

> Effective, long-lasting improvements to processes are not made by firefighting individual time-line conditions that are beyond a desired objective.

Effective, long-lasting improvements to processes are not made by firefighting individual time-line conditions that are beyond a desired objective; that is, approximately 2 percent of this time for this example. Process improvements are made by examining all output data collectively to determine what should be done differently in the overall process, as opposed to assessing the points that are beyond the criteria as individual occurrences. This can be accomplished through a P-DMAIC project.

6.3   Example 6.2: Tabular Red–Yellow–Green Metric Reporting Alternative

Table 2.5 presented a red–yellow–green graphic scorecard/dashboard report out for a continuous response that has a criterion.

The following observations were made from the chart for finance metric B, which had a target of 2.25 or higher. There were five red, two yellow, and six green occurrences:

Reiterating the IEE analysis process that will be followed below, the IEE scorecard/dashboard metric reporting process uses the following procedure:

1. Assess process predictability.
2. When the process is considered predictable, formulate a prediction statement for the latest region of stability. The usual reporting format for this statement is as follows:
   a. When there is a specification requirement: nonconformance percentage or DPMO.
   b. When there is no specification requirement: median response and 80 percent frequency of occurrence rate.

Applying the IEE scorecard/dashboard metric reporting process to this data set yields:

1. As previously stated, the purpose of red–yellow–green charting is to stimulate improvements. Figure 6.2 provides an IEE assessment of how well this is accomplished (see Breyfogle (2008c) for chart-creation methods). This figure contains a control chart, probability plot, and histogram. As noted in the previous example, when there are no occurrences beyond the two horizontal lines (i.e., upper and lower control limits), no patterns, or data shifts, the process is said to be in control. Again, when this occurs, we have no reason to not believe that the up-and-down monthly variability is the result of common-cause variability; that is, the process is predictable. Since the process is predictable, we can consider past data from the region of stability to be a random sample of the future.
2. The histogram shown in Figure 6.2 is a traditional tool that describes the distribution of random data from a popula-

Effective long-lasting improvements to processes are not made by firefighting individual time-line conditions that are beyond a desired objective. Process improvements are made by collectively examining process data over the period of stability to determine what should be done differently overall. This can be accomplished through the execution of a P-DMAIC project.

tion that has a continuous response. However, it is difficult to determine from a histogram the expected percentage beyond a criterion. A probability plot is a better tool to determine the nonconformance percentage. In a probability plot, actual data values are plotted on a coordinate system where percentage *less than* is on the *y-axis.* The probability plot in Figure 6.2 provides an estimate that approximately 32.6 percent of future monthly reporting will be less than the lower-bound criterion, unless a fundamental process improvement is made or something else external to the process occurs. From this figure, we also observe that this percentage value is consistent with an estimated proportion below the 2.2 reference line in the histogram graph. This percentage is also similar to the percentage of red occurrences; that is, 5 out of 13. If this nonconformance percentage of 32.6 percent is undesirable, this metric would pull for project creation.

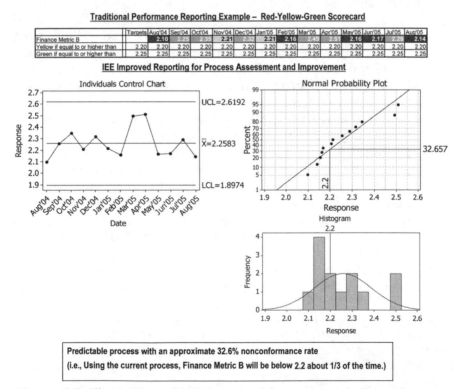

Figure 6.2: Illustration of IEE-improved finance metric B continuous-response reporting: Red-yellow-green (see Table 2.5) scorecard versus IEE reporting (Histogram included for illustrative purposes only).

6.4 IEE Performance Scorecard/Dashboard Metrics That Lead to the Right Activities

The example in the previous sections illustrate how simple goal setting does not necessarily yield improvements and, in fact, can lead to playing games with the numbers so that the company is negatively impacted. An IEE measurement-and-improvement infrastructure provides a solution to this problem.

Most first-tier companies use scorecard/dashboard metrics, which seem useful and claim to do the following:

- Provide a uniform view of a program or process across the organization.
- Force the organization to look at the forest instead of the trees; that is, report on the overall results of a process.
- Effectively and efficiently report the state of a process to those not intimately involved such as managers, peers in other organizations, and others.
- Provide a starting point for discussions on the key issues.
- Help to manage time in review meetings, since only the relevant issues are discussed.
- Provide a metric and any metric is better than no metric (*note*: this could be used to start non-value-added activity, which leads to ineffective resource utilization).

But think back on what comes out of these review meetings. These meetings typically have the following characteristics:

- A description of exceptions or problems.
- Half-baked plans to address both the problem and its consequences: shipments were late, not sure why, how to get on-time shipments, and how to mollify the customers who received late shipments.
- Too many problems: talking only about problems and the organization's apparent lack of ability to perform better makes for unhappy meetings.
- And most importantly, every meeting is the same; only the problems change. But there are always problems, always angst, always the need to fix the problem and the consequences of the problem, and always no real improvement.

Consider alternatively using 30,000-foot-level scorecard/dashboard metric reporting to achieve the following benefits:

- Reduced firefighting of common-cause problems as though they were special cause.
- Reporting process performance in terms that everyone understands; for example, the process is predictable with a two percent nonconformance rate that costs the business $200,000 monthly.
- Assess trends *before* they are classified as problems that need immediate attention.
- For statistically determined common-cause or special-cause problems, provides clear, specific direction for the process breakdowns. Benefits include the following:
    - Actionable activities are recognized.
    - Subprocess improvements can be measured and quantified.
    - Success is seen and rewarded in subsequent meetings when subprocesses are improved.
    - Over time, the overall process is not only under control, but also *improves.*

It is important to keep the following points in mind:

- Bad stress is when people feel they are not in control. Traditional dashboards show problems without a clear read on why or how to fix it.
- Good stress is when people feel that they have control over the situation. IEE provides a high-level process view highlighting areas that need fixing with actionable tools.

In an E-DMAIC structure, high-level enterprise-process analyses can provide metric goals and a structured improvement strategy that are truly aligned to business objectives and needs. The number of these metrics and value-chain goals from this analysis may be fewer than the number of current organizational metric-improvement objectives.

Improvement goal objectives determined at the 30,000-foot-level from an E-DMAIC analysis could be placed in employees' performance plans and reported as a scorecard/dashboard metric. Whether metric improvement goals are later met, and how well, would be assessed at the 30,000-foot-level for a statistically positive metric shift. Implementation of this methodology would be creating a system and culture where metric improvement needs pull for the creation of projects that have long-lasting benefits for the company.

The Sarbanes–Oxley (SOX) Act is legislation created in 2002 partly in response to the Enron and WorldCom financial scandals. SOX was created to protect shareholders and the public from enterprise-process accounting errors and fraud. In addition, it ensures a degree of consistency in access to information and reporting of it that could impact the value of a company's stock. IEE is in direct alignment with the initial spirit of SOX.

7

Enterprise Orchestration through IEE Value Chain Scorecards and Process Standardization that has Integrated Documentation

In both the E-DMAIC define phase and the P-DMAIC measure phase, it is advantageous to represent system structure and relationships using flowcharts. A flowchart provides a picture of the steps needed to create a deliverable. The process-flowchart document can maintain consistency of application, identify opportunities for improvement, and identify key process input variables (KPIV). It can also be very useful to train new personnel and to describe the activities expediently during audits. Benefits are maximized with processes are described and integrated throughout the organization.

This chapter describes a system for organizational process alignment with a no-nonsense performance metric system. The described Integrated Enterprise Excellence (IEE) methodology helps to stimulate the most appropriate behavior throughout the organization for the business as a whole.

7.1 Processes and Metrics

Every day we encounter devices that have an input and an output. For example, the simple movement of a light switch causes a light to turn on. Input to this process is the movement of the switch. Within the switch, a process is executed whereby internal electrical connections are made, and the output is a light turning on. This is just one example of an input–process–output (IPO), illustrated in Figure 7.1.

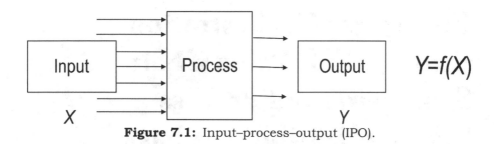

Figure 7.1: Input–process–output (IPO).

As users of a light switch, toaster, or radio, we are not typically interested in the mechanical details of how the process is executed. We typically view these processes as a black box. However, there are other processes with which we are more involved, for example, the process we use when preparing for and traveling to work or school. For this process, there can be multiple outputs such as arrival time, whether you experienced an automobile accident or another problem, and perhaps whether your children or spouse also arrived on time. The important outputs to processes are called key process output variables (KPOVs), critical to quality (CTQ) characteristics, or Ys.

> We might see much variability in the output of our process. We might then wish to examine why there is so much variability by consciously trying to identify the inputs to the process that can affect the process output.

For both black box and other processes, we can track output over time to examine the performance of the system. Inputs to processes can take the form of *inherent process inputs* (e.g., raw material), *controlled variables* (e.g., process temperature), and *uncontrolled noise variables* (e.g., raw material lots). For our example of going to work or school, consider that daily we quantified the difference between our actual and planned arrival times and then tracked this metric over time. For this measure, we might see much variability in the output of our process. We might then wish to examine why there is so much variability by consciously trying to identify the inputs to the process that can affect the process output. For reducing the variability of commuting time, we might list inputs to our process as departure time from home, time we got out of bed, traffic congestion during the commute, and whether someone had an accident along our route.

If we examine the inputs to our process, there are both controllable and uncontrollable, or noise, inputs. A controllable input might be setting the alarm clock, while an uncontrollable input is whether someone had an accident on our route that affected the travel time. By examining our arrival times, we might find that if we left the house 5 minutes earlier we could reduce our commute time by 25 minutes. For this situation, departure time is a KPIV that is an important X, which affects our arrival time. When this KPIV is controlled in our go-to-work or go-to-school process, we can reduce the amount of variability in our arrival time (KPOV).

Another tactic to reduce the variability of our arrival time is to change our process, so that we can reduce the commute time or make our process robust to withstand the effect of uncontrollable input variables. For example, we might change our travel route to work or school to avoid the high traffic hours of the day. This change could also reduce the likelihood of lengthy delays from accidents. We made our process robust with respect to accidents, which was a noise input variable.

There is always a process, even though it cannot be seen or is not standardized. Manufacturing processes are easy to see. We can simply follow the product. Processes are much more difficult to see in intangible business areas such as legal and financial.

Some managerial processes are beyond the scope of producing, distributing, or selling a product or service. These include budgeting, business planning, rewards and recognition, and process reporting. Middle management typically owns the responsibilities for design and implementation of these processes. These processes should help orchestrate the business toward efficiency and effectiveness, where everyone is going in the same direction toward meeting business objectives. When they are poor processes, the organization can become dysfunctional, which can result in much wasted effort and even business failure. Since the means of making improvement is through the process, understanding the process is crucial to making improvements.

Similarly, in business and other organizations we have processes or systems. For the process for going to work or school, the identification of inputs and potential process changes that positively impact our process output is not too difficult. Easy fixes can also occur within business processes when we view it systematically through an IEE strategy. However, identification and improvement systems for some business processes can be complex. For these situations, I view this search for KPIVs and process-improvement strategies as a mystery, where we uncovering clues, using a structured approach, that lead us to understand the process outputs.

Table 7.1 illustrates KPOVs (*Y*s) that a company could experience along with one, of perhaps many, associated KPIV (*X*s) for each of these processes.

These *Y*s are at various levels within an organization's overall system of doing business. One should note that the input to one process can be the output from another. For example, a described input for expense is work in progress (WIP), which is a high-level output from other processes.

Both customers and suppliers are involved in a process. This relationship is often expressed using a supplier–input–process–output–customer (SIPOC) diagram (see Breyfogle, 2008c).

In IEE an enterprise cascading measurement methodology (ECMM) can be created, which aligns metrics throughout the organization to the overall organizational needs. The tracking of these measurements, over time, can then pull for the creation of P-DMAIC or DFIEE/DFSS projects, which address improvement needs for common-cause variability for the process output. Through this pragmatic approach, where no games are played with the numbers, organizations have a systematic way to

Table 7.1: KPOVs (Ys) with a KPIV (X) for Each.

	Ys or KPOVs	Xs or KPIVs
1	Profits	Identification and exploitation of enterprise constraint
2	Customer satisfaction	Out of stock items
3	Enterprise goal	Development of improvement strategies from enterprise analysis
4	Expense	Amount of WIP
5	Production cycle time	Amount of internal rework
6	Defect rate	Invoices returned because they were sent to the wrong department
7	Critical dimension on a part	Process temperature

improve both their bottom line and customer satisfaction. This system is much more than a quality initiative – it is a business way of life.

The IEE system uses 30,000-foot-level scorecard/dashboard metric terminology to describe a high-level view for KPOV (CTQ, or *Y* variable) responses. This high-level, in-flight airplane view for operational and project metrics has infrequent subgrouping/sampling so that short-term variations, which might be caused by KPIVs, will result in charts that view these perturbations as common-cause issues. A 30,000-foot-level individuals control chart (see Breyfogle (2008c) for chart-creation methods) can reduce the amount of organizational firefighting when used to report operational metrics.

An alignment and management of metrics may be implemented throughout the organization so that there is an orchestration of the right activity being done at the correct time. Meaningful measurements are statistically tracked over time at various functional levels of the business. This leads to an ECMM, where meaningful measurements are statistically tracked over time at various functional levels. In this system, there is an alignment of important metrics throughout the organization. This alignment extends from the satellite-level business metrics to high-level KPOV operational metrics, which can be at the 30,000-foot-level, 20,000-foot-level, or 10,000-foot-level (infrequent subgrouping/sampling), to KPIVs at the 50-foot-level (frequent subgrouping/sampling). This metric system helps organizations run the business, so there is less firefighting and it has a pull system for the creation and execution of projects whenever operational metric improvements are needed.

7.2 Flowcharting

A flowchart provides a complete pictorial sequence of a procedure to show what happens from start to finish. Applications include procedure documentation, manufacturing processes, work instructions, and product-development steps. Flowcharting can minimize the volume of documentation, including ISO 9000 documentation.

Figure 7.2 exemplifies the form of a process flowchart and includes frequently used symbols to describe the activities associated with a process chart.

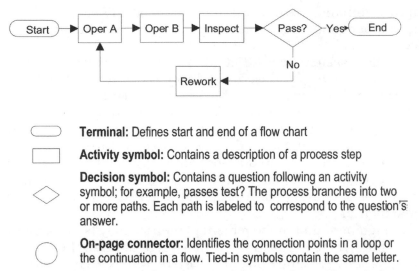

Terminal: Defines start and end of a flow chart

Activity symbol: Contains a description of a process step

Decision symbol: Contains a question following an activity symbol; for example, passes test? The process branches into two or more paths. Each path is labeled to correspond to the question's answer.

On-page connector: Identifies the connection points in a loop or the continuation in a flow. Tied-in symbols contain the same letter.

Figure 7.2: Process flowchart and frequently used symbols.

An arrowhead on the line segment that connects symbols shows the direction of flow. The conventional direction of a flowchart is top to bottom or left to right. Usually the return-loop flow is left and up. When a loop feeds into a box, the arrowhead may terminate at the top of the box, at the side of the symbol, or at the line connecting the previous box. The use of on-page connectors can simplify a flowchart by reducing the number of interconnection lines.

An illustration of a process can proceed down the left side of a page, have a line or on-page connector that connects the last box of the left column with the first box of the right column, and continue down the right side of a page. Boxes should be large enough to contain all necessary information to describe who does what. Notes can contain nondirective information.

When creating a flowchart, consider and describe the purpose and the process to be evaluated. Define all steps to create a product or service deliverable. This can be done in several different ways. One common approach is to conduct a meeting for those familiar with a process. The team then describes the sequence of steps on a wall or poster chart using one self-stick removable note for each process step. With this approach, the team can easily add or rearrange process steps. After the meeting, one person typically documents and distributes the results.

I prefer to use another approach when documenting and defining new processes. While conducting a team meeting to either define or review a process, I use a process-flowcharting computer program in conjunction with a projector that displays an image on a screen. This approach can significantly reduce time, greatly improve accuracy, and dramatically diminish the reworking of process description. Process-flowcharting programs offer the additional benefit of easy creation and access to subprocesses. These highlighted subprocesses can be shown by double-clicking with a mouse.

Flowchart creation using software offers flexibility, as illustrated in Figures 7.4–7.7, which we will discuss later. A value stream mapping (VSM), as illustrated in Figure 7.6, can be integrated with the flowcharting of process steps. A VSM is useful to show both physical product flow and information flow.

7.3   Enterprise-Process Value Chain

Most organizations create an organizational chart and then manage through that chart. However, the enterprise-process customer can experience something quite different; that is, the impact from the fundamental flow of what is being done. The steps of the value chain capture at a high level what we do and how we measure what is done. The metrics that are aligned to steps of the value chain need to be tracked and reported at the satellite-level or 30,000-foot-level as a scorecard/dashboard. The shading on two functional steps in Figure 7.3 indicates these steps have drill-down procedures, as described in the next section.

> Most organizations create an organizational chart and then manage through that chart. However, the enterprise process customer can experience something quite different; that is, the impact from the fundamental flow of what is being done.

An organizational value chain can begin at the corporate level, site level, or other level throughout the company. As previously demonstrated, this value chain can also become the linkage to all standard operating procedures and processes. An example of a partially constructed value chain is shown in Figure 7.3. Notice how the main flow describes at a high level what the organization does, where separate functions such as Human Resource (HR) and Information Technology (IT) could be described as separate entities. In all cases, created metrics describe what is important to the business and where these metrics should address Lean

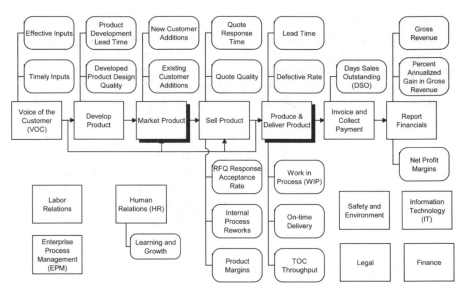

Figure 7.3: Value chain with scorecard/dashboard metrics. Shaded areas designate processes that have subprocess drill-downs.

E-DMAIC issues, such as quality, waste, lead time, and total costs.

As was noted earlier, in the early 1990s the balanced scorecard was introduced, which addressed at the same time finance, customer, internal business processes, and learning and growth. Achieving scorecard balance is important because if you don't, you could be giving one metric more focus than another, which can lead to problems. For example, when focus is given to only on-time delivery, product quality could suffer dramatically to meet shipment dates. However, you have to be careful in how you achieve this balance. A natural balance is much more powerful than one that forces an inappropriate structure throughout the organization. All the characteristics of the balanced scorecard are naturally covered in this value chain, noting that learning and growth was assigned to HR.

A value chain can be created so that a simple double-click on a performance metric will present the 30,000-foot-level or satellite-level scorecard/dashboard metric. This performance-metric format can lead to improved behavior over the previously described metric reporting systems in Sections 2.3, 2.6, and 2.7. Cunningham and Oriest (2003) describe metric guidelines as:

- Support the company's strategy.
- Be relatively few in number.
- Be mostly nonfinancial.
- Be structured to motivate the right behavior.
- Be simple and easy to understand.
- Measure the process, not the people.
- Measure actual results versus goals.
- Do not combine measures of different things into a single index.
- Be timely; weekly, daily, or hourly.
- Show trend lines.
- Be visual.

The following Figures later present various aspects of the value chain:

- Figures 7.4–7.7 illustrate how value chain linkage of processes and procedures creates an easy accessible documentation repository.
- Figure 7.8 illustrates where organizationally the overall E-DMAIC process management orchestration can reside in the value chain, noting that this is where existing enterprise process analysis and improvement procedures could reside.
- Figure 7.9 exemplifies value chain linkage with organization's satellite-level metrics.
- Figures 7.10–7.12 exemplifies value chain linkage with 30,000-foot-level functional performance metrics.

The reporting of business metrics at the satellite-level is included in the last value-chain step. These business metrics are to reflect important business financial metrics, where this satellite-level reporting does not have calendar boundaries such as year and month. Examples of satellite-level metrics are as follows:

- Gross revenue
- Net profit margin
- Profit
- Earnings before interest, depreciation, and amortization (EBIDA)
- Voice of the customer (VOC).

Operational metrics are also reported throughout the value chain. As in hoshin kanri, each function in a value chain could have a generic mission definition that addresses quality, cost, and delivery. The measurements for each generic mission should not change as a function of the overall organization mission changes. However, goals for these metrics could change depending on business inputs and VOC. E-DMAIC analyses can provide insight as to where directed improvement efforts would have the most benefit to the overall enterprise. Improvement measurement needs would pull for project creation (see Breyfogle, 2008b).

> These metrics provide a no-nonsense scorecard/dashboard business tracking at the 30,000-foot-level. They assess how the organizational functions are performing over time relative to predictability, along with appropriate prediction statements ...

These metrics provide no-nonsense scorecard/dashboard business tracking at the 30,000-foot-level. They assess how the organizational functions are performing over time relative to predictability, along with appropriate prediction statements; that is, functional-process capability/performance metric statements.

These VOC internal and external metrics need to have an owner responsible for performance of these functions and meeting of agreed to metric goals. Value-chain scorecard/dashboard metrics that should be reported in the 30,000-foot-level metric format, as opposed to the tables and chart formats previously described, include the following:

- Defective and defect rates.
- Lead times.
- Number of days sales outstanding (DSO).
- Customer satisfaction and loyalty.
- On-time delivery.
- Unplanned downtime as percentage of total available time.
- Injury rate; total employee work hours between injuries.
- Medical costs per employee.
- Lost-time accidents as a percentage of total possible employee work time.
- Number of days from promise date.

- Number of days from customer requested date.
- Raw material inventory.
- WIP inventory.
- Finished goods inventory.
- Performance to customer demand rate.
- Sales per employee.
- Market share.
- Absenteeism as percentage of workforce.
- Product-development lead time.
- Operating cost as a percentage of sales.
- Research and development as a percentage of sales.
- Percentage of sales from new products.
- Capital investment as percentage of sales.
- Working capital as a percentage of sales.

7.4   Value Chain Drill-Downs

A readily available format may be created to describe each step's value creation, so that standard operating procedures, process inputs, and other factors are easily understood.

Organizations have procedural documents; however, there is often no single repository for locating procedural flowcharts and associated documents. The following web-based value chain with drill-downs addresses this issue, where a simple click on a value-chain step leads to its drill-down subprocess, attached documents, or website options.

Figure 7.4 uses Figure 7.3 to illustrate the creation of a subprocess, which can have procedural linkages and further subprocess drill-downs. All new IEE project procedures and business-process-improvement events (BPIEs) should be linked to the value chain. Figure 7.5 illustrates how "swim lanes" can be used to describe different subprocess procedures.

Figure 7.6 shows the linkage of VSM to the value chain. VSM can address both product and information flow, along with the reporting of lead time versus value-added time (see Breyfogle, 2008b). From this model, we can also run simulations to address what-if possibilities. The customer value stream is very important since it is a basis for organizational improvements.

Figure 7.7 shows how a simple value-chain click can lead to a procedural document and website option linkage.

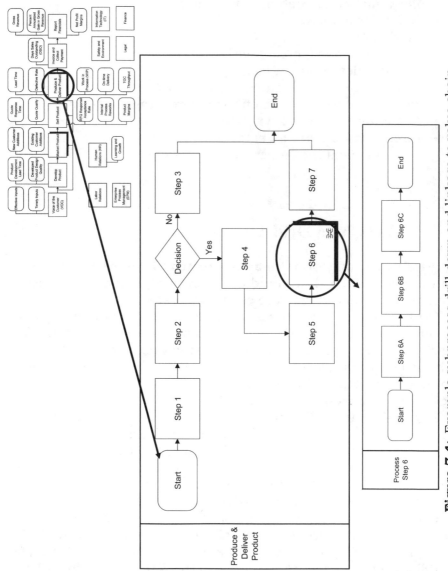

Figure 7.4: Example subprocess drill-down and linkage to value chain.

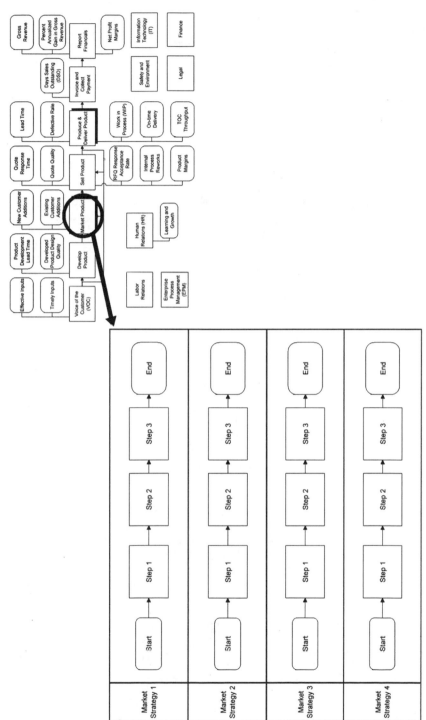

Figure 7.5: Example subprocess swim-lane drill-down.

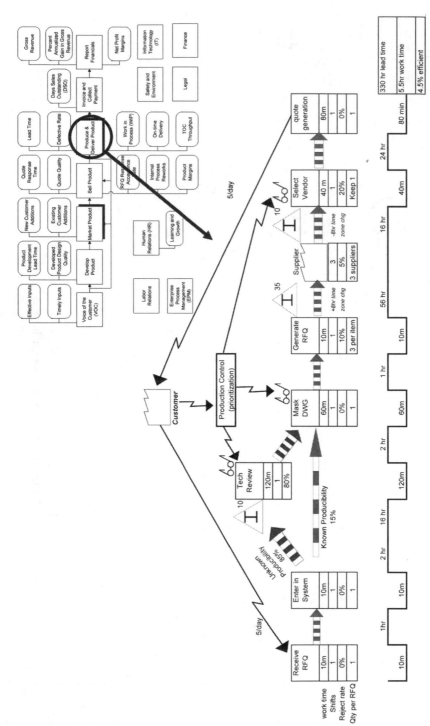

Figure 7.6: Example subprocess VSM drill-down.

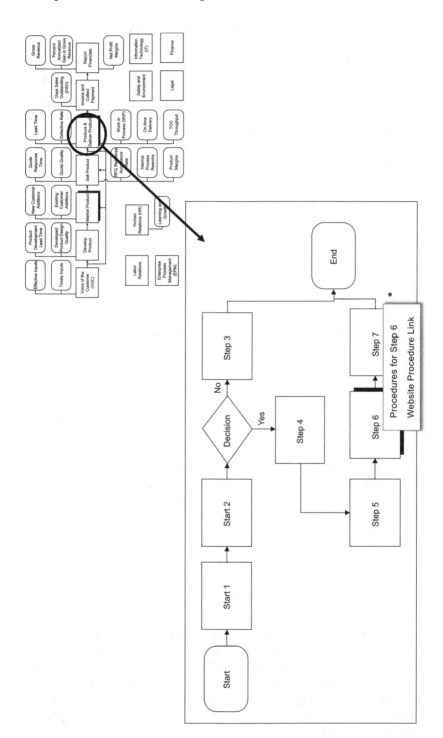

Figure 7.7: Example linkage in a process step.

* Options after clicking on Step 6

7.5   Enterprise Process Management (EPM)

It is unfortunate that many companies compile VOC data without having an overall plan that addresses what they will do with the data once they receive it. Organizations need a sustainable governance system for not only capturing customer data but also for conducting competitive new-product-development analyses, reporting metrics, creating strategic plans, and so forth. Organizations need a sustainable system that captures KPIVs and translates this input into both real products or services and actionable items.

As organizations move forward, it can be healthy to honestly assess the effectiveness of existing systems based on auditable results. This assessment can address whether these systems are being executed consistently and effectively, where executed procedures are part of an overall procedural repository. Often there are indications for improvement opportunities.

> Rather than having a governance model that addresses initiatives as separate entities, a value chain Enterprise Process Management (EPM) function can be created that orchestrates this system.

Rather than having a model for governance that addresses initiatives as separate entities, a value-chain enterprise process management (EPM) function can provide orchestration to this system. The EPM function, as shown in the value chain in Figure 7.8, is responsible for integrating, overseeing, and improving the execution of these processes using an E-DMAIC roadmap.

The EPM function can orchestrate the integration of existing enterprise procedures with the appropriate overall E-DMAIC functions described in this book, where ownership assignments can be made (see Breyfogle, 2008b). In a one-week workout, we have helped the organizations to successfully create the drill-down structure for each of the enterprise-process steps shown in Figure 7.8. The detail for each of these steps is refined over time.

The integration of the E-DMAIC methodologies with existing procedures can lead to an improved overall enterprise system, which is more data driven and sustainable. Improved measurements from this implementation can lead to a significant reduction in waste and reduce firefighting activities. Activity checks and balances that ensure continuing improvements through timely project completions that are part of the E-DMAIC control phase (see Breyfogle, 2008b).

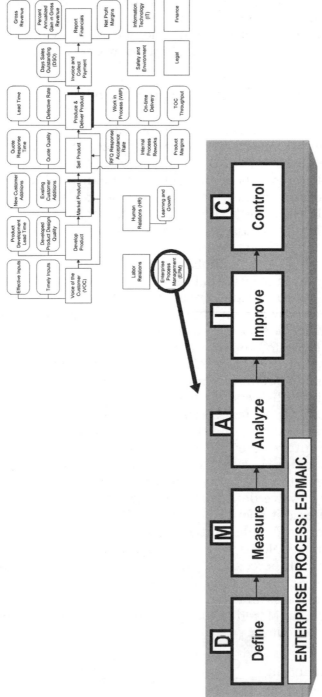

Figure 7.8: Enterprise process management (EPM) drill-down.

This EPM function implementation can lead to the creation of an enterprise system that consistently allows a company to retain its current customer base with no added expense, while maximizing its resources to attract and secure new ones.

7.6   Example 7.1: Satellite-Level Metrics

This example gives focus to the interpretation and use of satellite-level metrics. The mechanics of creating these charts is described in Breyfogle (2008c).

We want to satisfy the stakeholders with our products and services. To accomplish this, we need to define and observe key metrics and indicators. Let's start with the financials, which provide a business-health picture of how well objectives and stockholder expectations are being met.

Organizations often establish annual gross-revenue growth-and-profit-margin objectives. Earlier it was illustrated that simply focusing on quarterly numbers often leads to the wrong activities. This example provides an alternative system-focused methodology that can provide more timely information on how good performance is relative to business goals.

Consider that the satellite-level metrics for Acme Medical are gross revenue, percentage annual gain in gross revenue, and net-profit margins. The report out of these satellite-level metrics in Figure 7.9 shows a time-series plot of monthly gross revenue. The reader should note that no curve has been fitted to this line for making future-revenue projections. Time-series projections can be very dangerous. Building an accurate time-series model requires a great deal of data. Because it would take one year to capture only twelve data points, this analysis could easily miss a timely statement about nonlinearity or a flattening of a growth curve. Because no statement was made relative to predictability, extrapolations could be very deceiving.

The 12-month percentage gain in gross revenue (GR; monthly reporting) is determined by calculating the annual percentage gain as if the yearly financial statements were closing that month. For example, a March 2008 percentage-gain point would be determined as follows:

$$\begin{array}{l}\text{GR \% annual gain} \\ \text{plot point for 3/08}\end{array} = \frac{GR_{[4/1/07 \text{ to } 3/31/08]} - GR_{[4/1/06 \text{ to } 3/31/07]}}{GR_{[4/1/06 \text{ to } 3/31/07]}} (100)$$

If a goal is to increase annual gross-revenue growth, detecting a process shift can take some time. However, this tracking procedure is in true alignment with the organizational annual-revenue-growth goal statement and can provide a monthly feedback assessment on the impact of efforts to achieve this goal.

With this form of reporting, management should not be reacting to the up-and-down control chart variability as though it were special cause. This does not mean that one should ignore the variation and simply talk it away as common-cause variability. What it does mean is that we do not react either positively or negatively to individual common-cause datum points; that is, we would examine the data collectively. If the numbers were down below what is desired, focus would be given to process-improvement effort, as opposed to spending a lot of time explaining what happened last month.

A detailed interpretation of the annualized percentage gain in gross revenue and profit margins plots shown in Figure 7.9 using the IEE scorecard/dashboard metric reporting process is:

1. Assess process predictability.
2. When the process is considered predictable, formulate a prediction statement for the latest region of stability. The usual reporting format for this statement is the following:
    a. When there is a specification requirement: nonconformance percentage or DPMO.
    b. When there is no specification requirement: median response and 80 percent frequency of occurrence rate.

An interpretation of the *annual-gross-revenue-growth plots* shown in Figure 7.9 using this process follows:

1. A control chart test on the annual-gross-revenue data indicated a shift about May 2002. Perhaps another company was acquired at this time. Since then, the process has experienced only common-cause variability. Even though the control chart appears to have some trends from this point in time, the rules of control charting would have us conclude that the process is now predictable.
2. From the probability plot, we estimate that since May 2002 a monthly median of 27.2 percent and an 80 percent occurrence frequency of 25.2 to 29.3 percent has occurred; that is, we expect that 80 percent of the future monthly reporting will be between these two percentages.

Traditional Performance Measure of Success (NEXT Quarter or Year-End Financial Statement)

IEE Improved Reporting for Process Assessment and Improvement

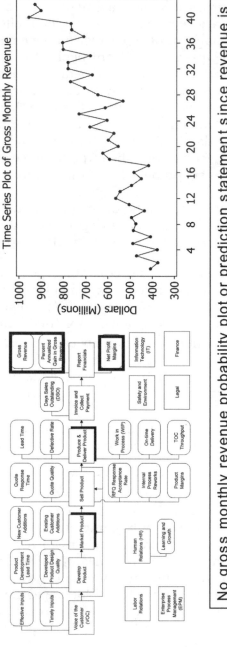

No gross monthly revenue probability plot or prediction statement since revenue is not predictable

Figure 7.9: (Part A) Comparison of traditional performance reporting with an IEE value-chain satellite-level scorecard/dashboard report.

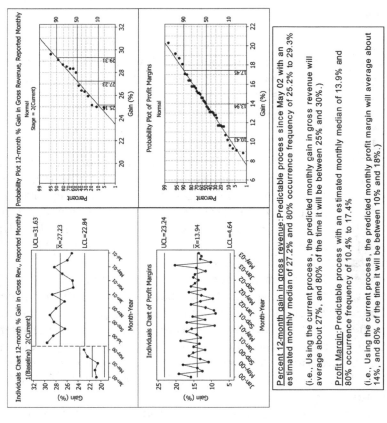

Figure 7.9: (Part B) Comparison of traditional performance reporting with an IEE value-chain satellite-level scorecard/dashboard report. Stage 1 (Baseline) and Stage 2 (New) process levels are designated are at the top of the graphs.

An interpretation of *profit-margin plots* shown in Figure 7.9 using this process are as follows:

1. Even though the control chart of profit appears to have trends, the rules of control charting would have us conclude that the process was predictable.
2. From the probability plot, we estimate a monthly median of 13.9 percent and an 80 percent monthly occurrence frequency of 10.4 percent to 17.4 percent; that is, we expect that 80 percent of the future monthly reporting will be between these percentages.

After all value-chain metrics are collectively examined, realistic goals can be set to improve the satellite-level metrics. A strategy could then be created to improve these metrics, which is a part of the E-DMAIC process analyze phase. As part of this enterprise decision-making process, areas thought to drive higher net-profit margins might be the reduction of defects and the creation of a new product line.

Specific goals can be established for improvements to the 30,000-foot-level scorecard/dashboard metrics. The 30,000-foot-level metric's owners would be responsible for making targeted improvements in the allotted time frame, for example, shift the process mean to the desired goal in 6 months. For the 30,000-foot-level metric to improve its level of performance, a fundamental improvement is needed in the process.

These metric improvement needs would pull for P-DMAIC project creation. Managers would then assign black belts or green belts to these projects who would follow the IEE project-execution roadmap described in Breyfogle (2008c). Since these managers are measured against the success of the metric shift, they will want to have frequent updates about the status of the project. The overall system that accomplishes this is part of the E-DMAIC analyze and improve phases.

One should note that this form of management focuses on improving the systems of doing things, as opposed to firefighting the process common-cause ups and downs or targeting tabular outputs that do not meet expectations, for example, red–yellow–green metric reporting.

This E-DMAIC reporting at the satellite-level and 30,000-foot-level can lead to a very positive governance model that moves organizations toward achieving the three Rs of business: everyone doing the Right things and doing them Right at the Right time. This is in contrast to a business governance model that encourage the executive team to do whatever it takes to achieve the next calendar-based financial target; that is, trying to manage the Y output of a process rather than giving focus to improving the process or its X inputs, which either positively or negatively impact the Y output.

Many practitioners would be hesitant to present this type of satellite-level and 30,000-foot-level (later examples in this chapter) metric report-out to their management. This is understandable, since this report-out is probably quite different than what has been previously presented and requested.

For those readers who see the benefit in this type of reporting and do not know how to get their management's interest, I suggest using advocacy selling and stealth training techniques. For the advocacy selling portion of this strategy, you could describe the charts off-line to a leading-thinking influential person, who is on the executive team. After taking the time to understand the IEE reporting methodology off-line, he/she could then support the creation of an opportunity, where you give a short presentation to the executive team. In this presentation, you could select data sets from your business where you compare your current methods with the described IEE methodology.

Now comes the stealth training. During the meeting you should give focus to the prediction statement, which is highlighted at the bottom of the presentation slide. You should not make any statement about the graphs *per se*, which is the stealth training portion of this presentation. What you want is someone to ask a question about the charts and variation swings. In most of these type meetings, someone will ask about the data variability that is conveyed in the charts.

When responding to this and other initial questions, don't try to give too much initial explanation – more detailed information can come in another presentation. You might simply say that all the up-and-down motion in the control chart is common-cause variability, which indicates that the process is predictable. Pointing now to the probability plot you could then show how the prediction statement was determined.

I suggest that you also have a slide that compares this IEE report out methodology to your traditional reporting methodology, which makes no prediction statement. During this presentation you might be able to demonstrate that your organization's many firefighting skirmishes have not really fixing much, if anything, long term.

I have had practitioners say that there is no way that their management would ever accept satellite-level and 30,000-foot-level reporting. However, these practitioners did try and now they say that their management is requesting this form of reporting.

7.7 Example 7.2: 30,000-Foot-Level Metric with Specifications

This example focuses on the interpretation and use of 30,000-foot-level metrics. The mechanics of creating these charts is described in Breyfogle (2008c).

Let's say that on-time delivery is considered as one of the greatest customer satisfiers to sales of products and services in Acme Medical's business value chain. This example provides a high-level view of the output from IEE 30,000-foot-level scorecard/dashboard metric reporting. For the purpose of illustration, the following data were randomly generated from a normal distribution.

In Acme Medical's value chain, the on-time delivery 30,000-foot-level scorecard/dashboard metric performance was tracked by randomly selecting one shipment weekly. Results from this analysis are shown in Figure 7.10, where +1 indicates one day late and −1 indicates one day early.

A detailed interpretation of this figure follows from the IEE scorecard/dashboard metric reporting process:

1. Assess process predictability.
2. When the process is considered predictable, formulate a prediction statement for the latest region of stability. The usual reporting format for this statement is the following:
   a. When there is a specification requirement: nonconformance percentage or DPMO.
   b. When there is no specification requirement: median response and 80 percent frequency of occurrence rate.

Interpretation of Figure 7.10 using this process:

1. Even though the control chart in Figure 7.10 appears to have trends, the rules of control charting would have us conclude that the process was predictable. As a reminder, these data were randomly generated and all variability was due to chance.

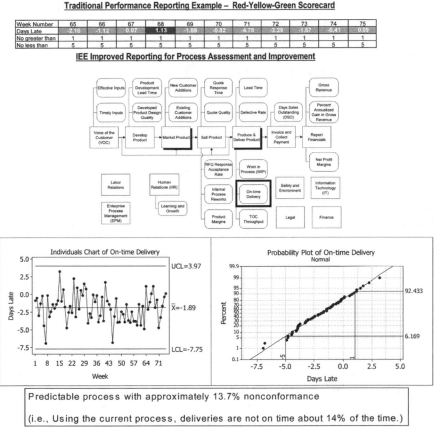

Figure 7.10 area:

Traditional Performance Reporting Example – Red-Yellow-Green Scorecard

Week Number	65	66	67	68	69	70	71	72	73	74	75
Days Late	-2.16	-1.12	0.07	1.13	-1.88	-0.82	-4.78	-3.29	-1.67	-0.41	0.09
No greater than	1	1	1	1	1	1	1	1	1	1	1
No less than	5	5	5	5	5	5	5	5	5	5	5

IEE Improved Reporting for Process Assessment and Improvement

Predictable process with approximately 13.7% nonconformance

(i.e., Using the current process, deliveries are not on time about 14% of the time.)

Figure 7.10: Comparison of traditional performance reporting with an IEE value chain 30,000-foot-level on-time delivery performance score-card/dashboard report. The traditional performance reporting example contains the most recent eleven data points.

2. The agreed-to shipping requirement was that shipments were not to be late (i.e., >+1.0) and no earlier than 5 days (i.e., −5.0) from their due date. The value-chain manager responsible for producing and delivering the product is responsible for this metric relative to current level of performance maintenance and any desired improvements. Acme's current performance and predicted future performance is that about 6.1 percent of all shipments will be earlier than the agreed-to date and about 7.6 percent of all shipments will be later than the agreed-to date (100−92.433=7.567 rounded off). This leads to the expectation that about 13.7 percent (6.1+7.6) will be either earlier or later than the agree-to delivery date.

Often, on-time-delivery metrics are reported as attribute data; that is, each shipment was received within the agreed-to time interval or not. It is hoped that the reader will appreciate the value of using the above continuous-response data-analysis approach over attribute reporting. With continuous data, much more insight is gained with a significantly smaller sample size. As illustrated in the example above, we not only estimate the proportion of shipments that are both early and late but we also describe the distribution of delivery times.

Using control charting rules, we have no reason to infer that the apparent short-term trends in the 30,000-foot-level control chart were from chance and should not be reacted to as individual values. Long-lasting improvements to this metric can be made through fundamental process changes.

When all value-chain metrics are collectively examined in the E-DMAIC analyze phase, this metric could be chosen as one that needs improvement because of its anticipated impact on gross-revenue goals, net-profit improvement goals, or customer retention. If this were the case, this metric would be creating a pull for project creation. The owner of this "produce and deliver product" metric would be responsible for making the targeted improvements in the allotted time frame, for example, shifting the process mean to the desired goal in 6 months. This manager would then assign a black belt or green belt to the project, where he/she would follow the IEE project-execution roadmap described in this book. Since this manager is measured against the success of the metric shift, he will want to have frequent updates about the status of the project.

Note how this form of management focuses on improving the systems of doing things, as opposed to firefighting the common-cause ups and downs of processes or point tabular values that do not meet expectations, such as red–yellow–green metric reporting.

7.8   Example 7.3: 30,000-Foot-Level Continuous Response Metric with No Specifications

This example gives focus to the interpretation and use of 30,000-foot-level metrics. The mechanics of creating these charts is described in Breyfogle (2008c).

Days sales outstanding (DSO) is important to business cash flow in the Acme's business value chain. This example gives a high-level view of the output from this 30,000-foot-level scorecard/dashboard metric reporting. The following data were randomly generated from a normal distribution. In this fictitious example, consider that some invoices had 90-day payment terms.

In Acme Medical's value chain, the DSO 30,000-foot-level metric performance was tracked by randomly selecting one invoice payment weekly and comparing the date of receipt to its due date. In this example, a + 1 would indicate that receipt was one day after the due date, while a − 1 would indicate that receipt was one day before the due date.

A detailed interpretation of this figure follows from the IEE scorecard/dashboard metric reporting process:

1. Assess process predictability.
2. When the process is considered predictable, formulate a prediction statement for the latest region of stability. The usual reporting format for this statement is:
    a. When there is a specification requirement: nonconformance percentage or defects per million opportunities (DPMO).
    b. When there are no specification requirements: median response and 80 percent frequency of occurrence rate.

Interpretation of Figure 7.11 using this process:

1. Even though the control chart in Figure 7.11 appears to have trends, the rules of control charting would have us conclude that the process was predictable. As a reminder, these data were randomly generated and all variability was due to chance.
2. Since there are no true specification requirements, a 50 percent and 80 percent frequency of occurrence reporting gives a good feel for what to expect from the process, including its variability. For this process, we estimate a median (50 percent frequency of occurrence) of about 4.8 days late with an 80 percent frequency of occurrence of 18.2 days early to 27.9 days late.

With this form of reporting, anyone, whether familiar with this process or not, has a general understanding of what to expect from it. To quantify better the impact of this tardiness, we can also report the impact in financial terms, such as a cost of doing nothing differently (CODND) metric.

As in the previous example, it is important to note that the apparent short-term trends in the 30,000-foot-level control chart

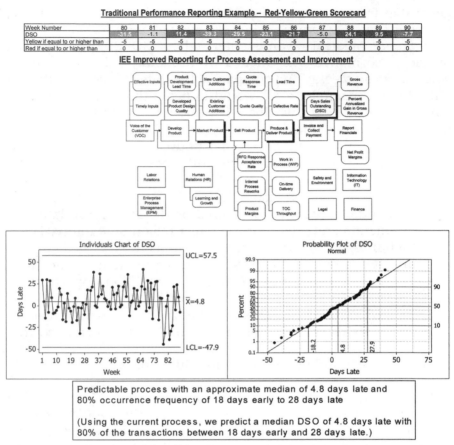

Figure 7.11: Comparison of traditional performance reporting with an IEE value chain 30,000-foot-level DSO performance scorecard/dashboard report. The traditional performance reporting example contains the most recent eleven data points.

were all from chance and should not be reacted to as an individual value. Long-lasting improvements to this metric are achieved only through fundamental changes to the process.

When all value chain metrics are collectively examined in the E-DMAIC analyze phase, this metric could be chosen as one that needs improvement because of its anticipated impact to gross revenue and net profit business goals. If this were the case, this metric would create a pull for a project creation. The owner of this "invoice and collect payment" metric would be responsible for making the targeted improvements in the allotted time frame, for example, shift process mean to an EIP goal in 6 months. The manager would then assign a black belt or green belt to this project, where he would follow the P-DMAIC execution roadmap described in this book. Since this manager is measured against the success of the metric shift, he will want to have frequent updates about the status of the project.

One should note how this form of management focuses on improving the systems of doing things, as opposed to fire fighting the common cause ups and downs of processes or point tabular values that do not meet expectations, for example, red–yellow–green metric reporting.

7.9   Example 7.4: 30,000-Foot-Level Attribute Response Metric

This example focuses on the interpretation and use of 30,000-foot-level metrics. The mechanics of creating these charts is described in Breyfogle (2008c).

As in our previous example, let's say that low defective rate is considered to be one of the greatest customer satisfiers influencing the sale of products and services in Acme's business value chain. This example gives a high-level view of the output from 30,000-foot-level scorecard/dashboard metrics reporting with randomly generated data. For illustration purposes, the following data were randomly generated from a normal distribution.

Acme Medical produced a certain amount of product daily. The defective rate 30,000-foot-level metric performance was tracked over time. Results from this analysis are shown in Figure 7.12. The "produce and deliver product" value chain manager is responsible for this metric relative to current level of performance maintenance and to any desired improvements.

A detailed interpretation of this figure follows from the IEE scorecard/dashboard metric reporting process:

1. Assess process predictability.
2. When the process is considered predictable, formulate a prediction statement for the latest region of stability. The usual reporting format for this statement is:
   a. When there is a specification requirement: nonconformance percentage or defects per million opportunities (DPMO.
   b. When there are no specification requirements: median response and 80 percent frequency of occurrence rate.

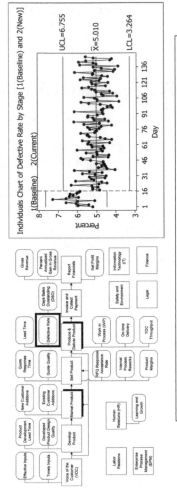

Figure 7.12 Comparison of traditional performance reporting with an IEE value chain 30,000-foot-level defective rate performance scorecard/dashboard report. Stage 1 (Baseline) and Stage 2 (New) process levels are designated and are at the top of the graphs. The traditional performance reporting example contains the most recent eleven data points.

Interpretation of Figure 7.12 using this process:

1. The individuals control chart of defective rate by stage indicates a process shift on day 16 establishing a new level of predictive performance.
2. Since we are tracking defective rate, we can use the mean response from this chart to estimate the current and future level of performance, which is about 5 percent defective rate. The centerline shift of 1 percent is an estimate of the process improvement on day 16.

Since day 16, this process has been experiencing common cause variability. These are best estimates of the performance of this process. If this process response is not satisfactory, something needs to be done to improve the process; that is, a pull for project creation.

An effort was made to improve this enterprise process step. A hypothesis test of the equality of the failure rate from Stage 1(Baseline) to Stage 2(Current) in Figure 7.10 indicates that significant improvement was made. The control chart was constructed to denote this shift, where the process has stabilized and now has a new process capability/performance metric. The current performance and predicted future defective rate is that of about 5 percent (5.01 rounded off). Since these are attribute data and assumed sub-group sizes are equal, the centerline of the stable process region is the estimated future defective rate.

It is important to note that the apparent short-term trends in the 30,000-foot-level control chart were all from chance and should not be reacted to as an individual value. Long-lasting improvements to this metric can be made through fundamental changes to the process.

> When all value chain metrics are collectively examined in the E-DMAIC analyze phase, this metric could be chosen as one that needs improvement because of its anticipated impact upon gross revenue and net profit improvement goals. If this were the case, this metric would be pulling for an improvement project creation.

When all the value chain metrics were collectively examined in the E-DMAIC analyze phase, this metric could have been chosen as one that needs improvement. If this were the case, a financial analysis would have indicated that a reduction in internal rework/reject rates would be an important step toward achieving a net profit margin business goal; that is, this metric improvement need would create a pull for project creation. The owner of this "produce and deliver product" metric would be responsible for making the targeted improvements in the allotted time frame, for example, shift process mean to the desired goal in 7 months. The manager would then assign a black belt or green belt to this project, where he would follow the project execution roadmap and checklists described in this book. Since this manager is measured against the success of the metric shift, he will want to have frequent project status updates.

8

Overcoming Business Constraints and Identifying Opportunities through Enterprise Analytics

Often in Six Sigma and Lean Six Sigma, focus is given to tools training for project execution. Little, if any, focus is given to how these tools can be applied at the enterprise level.

In addition, it is not uncommon for a company to claim they saved 100 million dollars with Six Sigma projects but no one can seem to find the money, even though the projects were validated by finance. Many companies who deployed Six Sigma can relate to this. The cartoon Dilbert even hits on issues like this.

I found one company to be working on many projects. After examining the overall system, one process step was identified as the constraint to the whole system. All the other projects were suboptimizing processes that had minimal impact on the financial big picture.

How can this type of problems be avoided? The Pareto principle, or 80 percent/20 percent rule, states that 80 percent of the effects come from 20 percent of the causes. How can we figure out the important vital few to work on, avoiding the trivial many?

This chapter highlights a system for identifying targeted focus areas that maximizes benefits to the enterprise as a whole using analytics.

8.1 Theory of Constraints (TOC)

The outputs of a system are a function of the whole system, not just individual processes. When we view a system as a whole, we realize that the output is a function of the weakest link. This is the constraint. If care is not exercised, we can be focusing on a sub-system that, even though improved, does not have an impact on the overall system output. Focus on the orchestration of efforts, not individual pieces, will optimize the overall system. Unfortunately, organization charts lead to workflow by function, which can result in competing forces within the organization. With TOC, systems are viewed as a whole and work activities are directed, so the whole system performance measures are improved. To illustrate this, consider the system shown in Figure 8.1. Similar to water flowing through a garden hose, the squeezing of one portion reduces flow volume as illustrated in Step 5.

Without considering the whole system, we might be spending a great deal of time and effort working on process Step 2 because this step is either not meeting its localized created target objectives relative to operating efficiencies, equipment utilization, and such. We note that improvements to process Step 2 would not significantly impact the overall system and could actually degrade the overall metrics if additional work in progress (WIP) is created from the improvements.

The TOC system chain extends from market demand through the organization chain to suppliers. Let's consider an example when this high-level view of the overall system is not addressed. An organization works at improving internal process efficiencies.

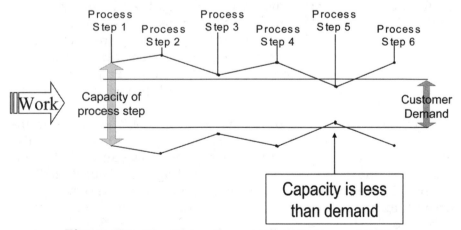

Figure 8.1: Identifying the overall system constraint.

Capacity then increases. Excess inventory is created because there is no sufficient demand. A discovery is made that the constraint is really the sales and marketing process. There are many ways to avoid this type of system using common sense and Lean tools.

Within an organization there are often constraints that we may or may not be aware of. Types of constraints that exist are market, resource, material, supplier, financial, and knowledge/competency. We need to look at the environmental rules or policies that drive the constraints.

8.2   Example 8.1: Theory of Constraints

In this example, I will use terms typically associated with manufacturing; however, the concepts apply equally to transactional processes.

A simple system is shown in Figure 8.2. Raw materials are processed through four component steps to produce a finished product. Each process step is an overall value stream link. The capacity of each step is described in the figure along with the market demand of 105 units per day. The goal is to make as much money as possible from the process.

From the examination of situation 1 in the figure, it is noted that the capacity of Step C is 75, which is less than the market demand of 105. Even though other steps in our value stream process may not be performing up to their equipment utilization and efficiency goals, focus should be given first to increasing the

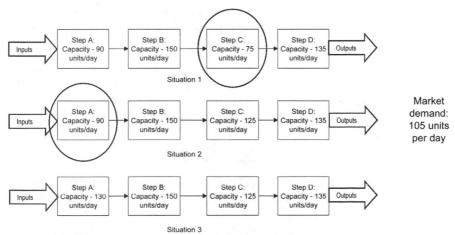

Figure 8.2: System constraint identification and resolution.

capacity of Step C. From this E-DMAIC analysis, Step C would be an opportunity for a P-DMAIC project.

Upon completion of the P-DMAIC project for Step C, the process then exhibited the characteristics of situation 2 shown in the figure. An analysis of this situation indicates that the constraint is now at Step A. From this E-DMAIC analysis, it would now be appropriate for a P-DMAIC project to focus on Step A.

Upon completion of a P-DMAIC project of Step A, the process then started exhibiting the characteristics of situation 3. An analysis of this situation indicates that all four steps of the process have enough capacity to meet the market demand. The internal system constraints relative to satisfying a market demand of 115 units per day have been removed. The constraint has moved outside the system to the market place. The next P-DMAIC project should focus on determining what can be done to increase product demand through improvements in the marketing and sales processes.

This example illustrated the importance of starting by analyzing the big picture to determine where efforts should focus when creating P-DMAIC projects. Loosing sight of the big picture can lead to the ineffective utilization of resources and the suboptimization of processes.

8.3   Total Quality Management and TOC

The implementation of traditional Total Quality Management (TQM) has often been implemented by dividing the system into processes and then optimizing the quality of each process. This approach is preferable to chasing symptoms; however, new problems can be created if the individual process is not considered in concert with other processes that it affects.

> The theory of constraints presented focuses on reducing system bottlenecks as a means to continually improve the performance of the entire system. Rather than viewing the system in terms of discrete processes, TOC addresses the larger systematic picture as a chain or grid of interlinked chains.

The theory of constraints (TOC) presented by Goldratt (1992) focuses on reducing system bottlenecks as a means to continually improve the performance of the entire system. Rather than viewing the system in terms of discrete processes, TOC addresses the larger systematic picture as a chain or grid of interlinked chains. The performance of the weakest link determines the performance of the whole chain. According to Goldratt, the vast majority of constraints results from policies of rules, training, and other measure, while few constraints are physical, such as machines, facilities, people, and other tangible resources. For example, a large portion of the highway road repair seems initially to be physically constrained by traffic flow. But the real constraint could also be government acquisition policy, which mandates the award of contracts to the lowest bidder. This drives contractors to the use of low-quality materials with shorter life in an effort to keep costs down and remain competitive.

TOC considers three dimensions of system performance in the following order: throughput (total sales revenues minus the total variable costs for producing a product or service), inventory (all the money a company invests in items it sells), and operating expense (money a company spends transforming inventory into throughput). Focus on these dimensions can lead a company to abandon traditional management cost accounting while at the same time causing an improvement in competitive price advantage.

8.4 Enterprise Data Analyses

ROI at the company level is a complex reflection of all individual activities over the reflected time period. I agree with Cunningham and Fiume (2003) who state, "If a company is constantly improving its processes, the results in ROI will come. This focus on improving the individual elements of the process, by eliminating waste and increasing velocity, has great impact on the bottom line, but only when we are not focused exclusively on that bottom line. The winners will be companies that focus on process first, not results."

Much insight can be achieved into what an organization can do to improve through a systematic analysis of the existing enterprise system and improvement possibilities with linkage to enterprise voice of the customer inputs. This analysis can involve the financials either directly or indirectly. In Davenport and Harris (2007) it is stated, "we discovered a significant statistical association between an organization's commitment to analytics and high performance. Companies with strong analytical orientations (those who answered with a 4 or 5 on all our questions) represented 25 percent of the sample (ninety-three companies), and their orientations correlated highly with financial outperformance in terms of profit, revenue, and shareholder return. In fact one of the strongest and most consistent differences between low- and high-performance businesses is their attitude toward, and application of analytics" Results from a study on importance of analytical orientation indicated:

- Have significant decision-support/analytical capabilities: low performers = 23%, high performers = 65%
- Value analytical insights to a very large extent: low performers = 8%, high performers = 36%
- Have above average analytical capability within industry: low performers = 33%, high performers = 77%
- Use analytics across their entire organization: low performers = 23%, high performers = 40%

Davenport and Harris (2007) provide the following illustrations of analytics use as part of an organization's enterprise:

- The value of Capital One's stock has grown two to four times faster than its largest competitors, increasing by 1000 percent over the past ten years. This performance outpaced the S&P 500 index by a factor of 10. Today, Capital One runs about three hundred experiments per business day to improve its ability to target individual customers. The company judges through these relative low-cost tests how successful products and programs would be before it engages in full-scale marketing.
- Progressive Insurance hunts the insurance markets and business models markets that have been ignored using conventional data analysis. Progressive's innovation led to the first real-time on-line auto insurance offering and rate comparisons. The company uses analytics in price setting to such an extent that it believes when companies offer lower rates they are taking on unprofitable customers.
- Marriott embeds analytics into several customer-facing processes. The most profitable customers are identified through its Marriott Rewards loyalty program so that marketing offers and campaigns can be targeted to them. Sophisticated Web analytics has led to a four billion dollar annual business through its on-line channel. The company, partly as a result of its wise use of analytics, has been named *Fortune*

magazine's most admired firm in its industry for seven straight years.

- Best Buy increases subsequent sales after an initial purchase through a predictive model. For example, a digital camera purchase could trigger a timely e-coupon for a photo printer.
- Sprint uses analytics to better understand customer life cycles. In this life-cycle model, 42 attributes are used to characterize interactions, perceptions, and emotions of customers from initial product awareness through service renewal/upgrade. This analytics is integrated into operational models to determine the best ways to maximize, over time, customer loyalty and spending.
- Google has a very large commitment to experimentation before making any search site change. Search engine algorithm changes need to pass through a test funnel and demonstrate substantial improvements with high quality.

Davenport and Harris (2007) highlight the three critical types of outcomes to measuring the performance of an initiative as behavior, processes and programs, and financial results. The financial results, which matter in the end, probably will not be achieved without focusing on intermediate outcomes; that is, the Xs in the relationship $Y = f(X)$.

- Behavior of employees, to a large extent, is a major driver of improved financial outcomes. For example, new analytical pricing strategies can require the behavior change of thousands of employees.
- Process and program changes are often required to improve results through fact-based analyses. For example, insights to deter the loss of wireless customers to another carrier need translation into actions, perhaps through a new training program for employees who face customers. The integration of analytics into business applications and work processes is a means to ensure that data-driven insights are incorporated into the business.
- Financial results may include goals to improve profitability or higher revenue. Cost savings are initially the most frequent justification for an analytical initiative because it is much easier in advance to specify how to cut costs. It is more difficult to predict and measure increased revenue; however, analytically models can be developed from small tests and pilot studies. With increased analytical maturity, organizations can become

more willing to invest in initiatives that have the target of exploiting growth and revenue-generating opportunities.

The insight gained from an effective enterprise analysis can enhance a company's strategic planning direction. At the enterprise level, there are many potential analysis paths. An approach to funnel down these many options is the scoping down of work through an enterprise brainstorming session. Wisdom of the organization tools that are a part of an improvement project execution roadmap could be used to facilitate this information collection process.

This wisdom of the organization work could then lead to hypothesis tests that would again utilize tools that are often associated with improvement project execution. The importance of getting to know your data through graphing and statistical analyses is an essential part of this overall process. People can get themselves into trouble when they just look at the results of a statistical analysis without plotting the data; that is, plotting and statistical analyses should both be used when appropriate. A systematic utilization of data analyses tools, such as those used in the P-DMAIC roadmap, helps orchestrate organizational strategic direction and improvement focus efforts. Areas to consider for this segmentation and analysis for differences and trends include:

- Sales source.
- Customer satisfaction/needs assessment.
- External force assessment; for example, changes in technology, competition, and government regulations.
- Internal force assessment; for example, core competencies, supplier and process assessments.

Let's now consider analyses' potentials for these areas. Example sales source assessments are:

- Statistical and graphic assessment of sales by sales personnel, department, managers, or regions.
- Pareto chart showing generated sales by customer/customer segment or product/service.
- Matrix showing sales or percent of sales from market segment versus product type.

The following example illustrates this form of analysis.

8.5 Example 8.2: Sales Personnel Scorecard/ Dashboard and Data Analyses

This example illustrates an Integrated Enterprise Excellence (IEE) alternative to traditional scorecard/dashboard reporting and analyses described in Sections 2.3, 2.6, and 2.7. More specifically, this example focuses on alternatives to the charting as described in Figures 2.1 to 2.3. Breyfogle (2008c) describes the mechanics to create the charts and conduct the analyses described in this example. The described analysis is on a small data set consisting of only five sales personnel; however, the described use of analytics could equally apply to much larger data sets for a variety of situations. This type of analytics in the E-DMAIC process can help both small and very large companies gain insight to what can be done to improve the efficiency and effectiveness of their business.

As was noted earlier, Figure 2.1 to 2.3 chart formats typically lead to *stories* about the past. The chart presentation format will dictate the presented *story* type. For example, the calendar boundaries in the Figure 2.3 bar-chart reporting format will surely lead to adjacent month and previous yearly month comparisons. Consider how accurate is a year-based reporting if something changed during the year? For example, if there was a fundamental sales process change in July, then we would be including old information with the latest information when examining annualized data in a pie chart. Wouldn't it be better to first identify if and when a change occurred and then either compare new to old process responses, or describe what is happening most recently?

Consider also, which interests us the most: the past or the future? Most often the response to this question is "the future." Reporting individual up-and-down historical movement or arbitrary-time-based comparisons do not provide insight to future process-output expectations, assuming that the process experiences no dramatic positive or negative change. However, if we could somehow estimate the future and we then don't like the resulting prediction, we gain insight to improvement focus opportunities; that is, the metric improvement needs pull for process improvement project creation. What is next described is an IEE metric reporting alternative that provides insight that these forms of reporting do not.

Figure 8.3 describes the results of a business area drill down of the gross revenue satellite-level metric. From this 30,000-foot-level

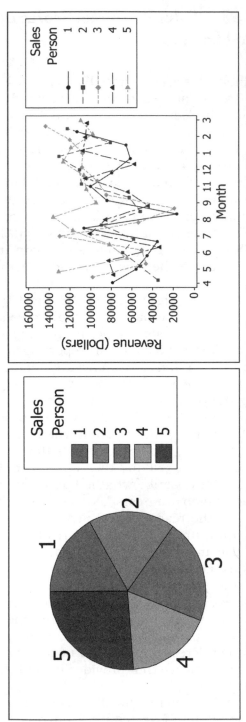

Figure 8.3: (Part A) Drill down to generated revenue from five sales persons, where the probability plot of individual salesperson revenue (see Part B) is from the last five months of stability.

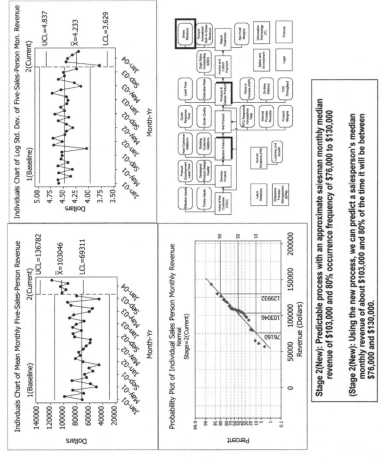

Figure 8.3: (Part B) Drill down to generated revenue from five sales persons, where the probability plot of individual salesperson revenue is from the last five months of stability.

scorecard/dashboard reporting analysis, we are able to identify a process shift in October 2003. This was when a team made a change and they could now see the impact from this change by the shift in the 30,000-foot-level control chart. The process reached an improved performance level, where the noted predictability statement reflects the last five months of stability.

A detailed interpretation of this figure follows from the IEE scorecard/dashboard metric reporting process:

1. Assess process predictability.
2. When the process is considered predictable, formulate a prediction statement for the latest region of stability. The usual reporting format for this statement is:
    a. When there is a specification requirement: nonconformance percentage or defects per million opportunities (DPMO).
    b. When there are no specification requirements: median response and 80 percent frequency of occurrence rate.

Interpretation of Figure 8.3 using this process:

1. Monthly subgrouping was chosen (see Glossary subgroup and infrequent subgrouping/sampling). Since there are multiple samples in the subgroups, two control charts are needed to assess within subgroup change over time. One control chart assesses whether the within subgroup mean response changes over time, while the other control chart address whether within subgroup variability changes over time. Breyfogle (2008c) describes why it is often best to track subgroup variability as the log of the subgroup standard deviation. For this example, the individuals control chart of the mean sales from the five sales persons indicates that the between subgroup mean response shifted and established a new level of predictive performance in October 2003. The individuals control chart of log standard deviation indicates that the between subgroup variability differences by sales person shifted and established a new level of predictive performance in October 2003.
2. From the probability plot of individual sales person monthly revenue, a prediction statement for the new level of process performance is that the approximate expected sales person's performance will be mean monthly revenue of

$103,000 and 80 percent frequency of occurrence by month of $76,000 to $130,000; that is, 80 percent of all individual monthly sales performances is expected to be between these two estimates.

Since October 2003, this process has been experiencing common cause variability. These are best estimates of the performance of this process. If this process response is not satisfactory, something needs to be done to improve the process; that is, a pull for project creation.

Figure 2.1 was included in Figure 8.3 for illustrative purposes to compare IEE 30,000-foot-level metric reporting against one form of traditional performance measures reporting. The reader should compare this report-out format to other options shown in Figures 2.2 and 2.3.

For example, consider the month–year bar chart reporting format illustrated in Figure 2.3. I suspect that the stories typically conveyed from a Figure 2.3 report-out format would be quite different from the conclusions presented during an IEE performance metrics report out. The stories that are conveyed from traditional reporting can often lead to resource-draining activities that have little value. For example, Joe might be told to investigate why September revenues are down when this reported value was from common-cause variation, not a special-cause condition.

I should point out that all data for this illustration were randomly generated, where the only process special cause occurrence was the process shift that occurred on October 2003. That is, except for this shift, all data up-and-down movements were what we could expect from common-cause variability.

In Figure 8.3, we note that the estimated mean monthly revenue for the five sales personnel is $103,046. Five times this mean response is greater than $500,000 mean monthly goal. Hence, our scorecard/dashboard prediction statement indicates that with the current process we expect to meet in the future the sales goals for the five salesmen. This statement also implies that any new higher goal for these five salesmen would require additional process change.

It should also be highlighted that when a process change does not occur on January 1 of a year, there will always be some

> ... when process input comparisons are assessed over an arbitrary interval such as annual, conclusions about the impact of these inputs can be distorted.

bridging of old and new process levels with annual reporting. This phenomenon does not occur with IEE reporting, since process capability/performance metric statements can be made at any point in time during the year.

In addition, when process input comparisons are assessed over an arbitrary interval such as annual, conclusions about the impact of these inputs can be distorted. To illustrate this, consider the pie chart in Figure 2.1, which compared monthly salesman revenue for the last 12 months. From this chart, it appears that salesman number five contributed more revenue than the other salesmen. I will now illustrate an IEE approach to make these assessments using both visualization and hypothesis statements in regions of stability.

An E-DMAIC analysis was to test the hypothesis that generated monthly sales from the five salesmen were equal. Instead of making an annual or some other arbitrary timeframe comparison, it is better to make comparisons within stable regions; for example, something could have changed between regions of stability. Figure 8.4 shows a dot plot visualization and a statistical analysis, which indicates a statistically significant difference in mean stage response. Because of this, each stage was analyzed separately.

Figures 8.5 and 8.6 show the visualization and statistical analysis for both stage 1(Baseline) and stage 2(Current). The marginal plot in each figure gives a visual representation of not only mean responses but also the accompanying variability that each sales person is delivering. In the Analysis of Means (ANOM) in these figures five hypothesis tests are present; that is, the mean of each salesperson was compared to the overall mean. When a plotted

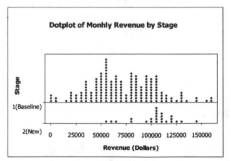
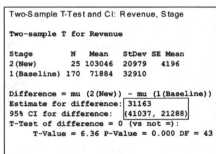

Conclusion: Significant difference in monthly sales personnel revenue. A per person best estimate for amount of monthly increased revenue is $31,200 (95% confidence interval of $21,300 and $41,000).

Figure 8.4: Visually and statistically comparing stage 1(Baseline) with stage 2(New) mean monthly sales personnel revenue.

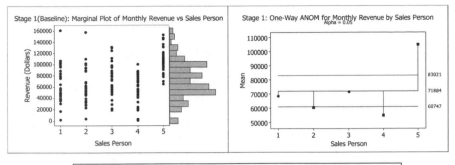

Figure 8.5: Stage 1(Baseline): Mean monthly revenue visualization and statistical analysis by sales person.

mean value in an ANOM plot is beyond one of the two horizontal decision lines, significance is stated at the charted risk probability, 0.05 in this case.

From the Figure 8.5 before change analysis (i.e., stage 1 – Baseline), it appears that salesperson number five generated significantly larger revenue than the other sales personnel. It appears that this larger revenue shifted the overall to a level that sales personnel number two and four were significantly lower than the overall mean.

From the after change Figure 8.6 analyses (i.e., stage 2 – Current) no salesperson mean revenue could be shown statistically different from the overall mean. It was noted that between stage 1(Baseline) and 2(Current) a project had changed the sales process of sales personnel 1, 2, 3, and 4 to be consistent with the most successful sales person; that is, number 5.

The reader should compare the thought process and conclusions from this analysis to the stories that would have been created from Figures 2.1–2.3. With the traditional reportout systems, there is no structured process to identify and react to the October shift.

To some readers, IEE performance metric reporting might look very complex with the additional fear that they would need to create a similar chart. These types of charts are not difficult to create with statistical software. Breyfogle (2008c) describes the mechanics of setting up these charts for a variety of situations. It is important to also realize that typically only a few people in the organization would need to create these charts. Managers and other leaders in the organization would only need to be able to

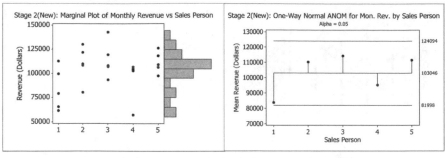

Figure 8.6: Stage 2: Mean monthly revenue visualization and statistical analysis by sales person

interpret the chart and create or address appropriate action plans from the charts.

This form of reporting and chart interpretation could transform the workplace culture from fire fighting to fire prevention. Management might now be asking Sue when her process improvement project is to be completed, since project completion is expected to decrease a mean process 30,000-foot-level metric response to a more desirable level. This is in contrast to a daily meeting in the company's war room where direction is given to Joe to "fix" the latest problem of the day.

8.6   Example 8.3: Making the Numbers Assessment

Cunningham and Fiume (2003) state, "compare these simple measures (customer service and inventory turns) with the one big hammer of a metric many companies use Make the Month. There are businesses that expend tremendous amounts of energy and resources toward the end of the month in one mad scramble to live up to whatever numbers were budgeted or promised. Make

There are businesses that expend tremendous amounts of energy and resources toward the end of the month in one mad scramble to live up to whatever numbers were budgeted or promised.

the Month might seem like a rather simple trap to avoid, but most typical results-oriented companies end up in the Make the month category. These businesses may get results in the short term – much as fad diets get results – but in most cases, the practice creates significant waste that can seriously damage a company in the long term.

How can we tell if a company has fallen into this trap? If we use the example of shipments, look at whether shipments reflect substantially more than 25 percent of monthly sales in the last week of a typical four-week month. If the answer is yes, Make the Month syndrome is at play. We have seen companies that regularly ship 50 percent to 80 percent of their monthly volume in the last week of the month. The resource implications of this are staggering. What are the resources, such as overtime, that are needed to process 80 percent of the volume in 25 percent of the time? Or, if the organization has staffed to comfortably handle that higher volume, then what amount of resources are sitting idle or involved in make-work activities the other 75 percent of the time?"

The financial impact from these situations could be quantified as the cost of doing nothing differently (CODND), which could then pull for an improvement project creation. An analysis of this situation might find that the sales department is offering discount incentives near month, or quarter, end to stimulate sales so that their numbers will be met. The question then becomes what could be done differently to address this behavior. Perhaps implementing an improvement project could create a new sales personnel compensation policy leading to improved sales throughout the month and discouraging previous end-of-the-month behavior, which had been adversely affecting manufacturing.

This form of detrimental business-making policy is not restricted to monthly manufacturing activities. Consider the resulting havoc when companies restrict travel near the year's end to meet annual budgeted or promised numbers. The impact from this type of policy can be very large; perhaps a customer was lost because a travel restriction impacted client servicing.

Organizations need to assess what changes are needed at the day-to-day process level to avoid short-term reactions to meet objectives that could have been arbitrarily set. A systematic assessment of data can provide insight into what should be done differently in policies and procedures to avoid future occurrences of these problem types. For this travel illustration, a company might find that significantly higher airline costs are occurring throughout the year because they are calling many last minute crisis travel meetings. This analysis result could then lead to the question: What can be done at the process level to reduce last minute travel meetings throughout the year? A Pareto chart of meeting types could pull for the creation of several process improvement projects.

9

Implementing the IEE System

The Integrated Enterprise Excellence (IEE) system has a project execution roadmap that truly integrates Lean and Six Sigma tools. In addition, the IEE system provides an enterprise roadmap that helps organizations not only to select better projects but also provides a no-nonsense integrated value chain measurement and analysis system that helps orchestrate day-to-day work activities and target system process improvement efforts.

The IEE system not only is a great system for viewing high-level operational business metrics but it also provides the tools to solve tough problems. For example, IEE techniques were used to help one company use design of experiments (DOE) to fix a 12-year-old biscuit crumbliness problem in a fast food chain. Another DOE fixed a major die breakage problem in an aluminum extrusion process which resulted in increased throughput for the entire plant. Another company was able to eliminate several warehouses because of improved process flows.

IEE is more of a business system than a do-project system such as Six Sigma and Lean Six Sigma. IEE takes Lean Six Sigma and the balanced scorecard to the next level.

Previous chapters described some traditional techniques and their challenges. This chapter describes the development of an IEE infrastructure.

147

9.1   Infrastructure

IEE is supported by a practitioner belt structure similar to that of traditional Six Sigma and Lean Six Sigma, where the value of maintaining and improving customer satisfaction must not be overlooked by organizational activities.

Black belts are a key part of the deployment infrastructure. Not only do selected black belts need to have the capability of learning and applying statistical methodologies, but they also need to be proactive people who are good at the soft skills needed while effectively working with others. Black belts will not only need to analyze information and use statistical techniques to get results, but also be able to work with others through mentoring, teaching, coaching, and selling others on how they can benefit from the techniques. In my experience, the most successful black belts possess the following skill set:

- *Fire in the belly*: They have an unquenchable desire to improve the way an organization does its business.
- *Soft skills*: They have the ability to work effectively with people in teams and other organizations.
- *Project management*: They have the ability to get things done well and on time.
- *System thinker*: They have an appreciation that work is accomplished through processes and that true long-lasting results are made through systematic improvements to these processes.
- *Multi-tasking*: They have no problem managing and scheduling several activities in the same time frame.
- *Unstructured environment management*: They have the ability to work in chaotic environments and create systems within these situations.
- *Big picture thinker*: They focus on aligning their efforts to impact the big picture. They avoid analysis paralysis.
- *Analytical skills*: They have correct and valid reasoning skills and are comfortable using mathematic techniques such as algebra.
- *Organizational navigation skills*: They can work around barriers without invoking higher authority.
- *Critical thinking skills*: They are skillful at conceptualizing, applying, analyzing, synthesizing, and evaluating information from multiple sources.

All these items have more linkage to inherent natural abilities than to teachable skill sets. It is not difficult to teach statistical methodologies if a person has good analytical skills, however, the lack of other personality traits can make it difficult to achieve benefits from the deployment. When implementing an IEE Business Strategy, organizations need to create a process for selecting black belt trainees that addresses innate talent as well as these skills.

Efforts to hire previously trained black belts are often not very successful. Hiring the right person who possesses the above skills is not an easy or mistake proof task. In addition, this new hire would need to fit into the organizational culture and know the internal structure for getting things done. Finally, one might ask how long we can anticipate this new hire will remain with the company. If the person is very good, headhunters might entice him to move onto another company – just after your company finally got him/her up to speed.

Alternatively, companies know which employees best fit the above profile. These employees already know the company protocol and how to get things done within its culture. With a little training and coaching, they can become very effective at implementing the system.

A rule of thumb for the number of black belts in an organization is 1 to 2 percent of the total number of employees. Black belts are supported technically through a master black belt and through the management chain of an organization by way of a champion. Individuals who are given IEE training to a lesser extent and support black belts are called green belts.

When an organization chooses to implement Six Sigma, Lean Six Sigma, or IEE, it is important that the organization hits the road running as soon as possible. It is important that the organization do it right the first time and not have a false start. It is important that internal organizational resources focus on creating the infrastructure and help with expediting results, not with the development of training materials.

Because of this, it is best to utilize an outside training/coaching company to get the organization started. This training/coaching company can help with setting up a deployment strategy, conducting initial training, and providing project coaching. The decision on which group is chosen can dramatically affect the success of its implementation. However, choosing the best group to help an organization implement Six Sigma can be a challenge. Some items for consideration are covered in Appendix Section A.3 of *Implementing Six Sigma* (Breyfogle, 2003).

This book focuses on using the E-DMAIC project execution roadmap to gain quick, repeatable results. The statistical community and others often comment that most procedures, which are suggested in these roadmaps, are not new. As a general statement, I do not disagree. However, the Six Sigma and Lean names have increased the awareness of upper level management to the value of using statistical concepts and nonstatistical concepts. The structure of the E-DMAIC roadmap provides an efficient linkage of the tools that help novice and experienced practitioners utilize both Six Sigma and Lean tools effectively.

Topics in Breyfogle (2008b) give focus to executing E-DMAIC steps, while Breyfogle (2008c) focuses on the execution of P-DMAIC steps. Many tools are applicable to both DMAIC methodologies; hence, in this series of volumes there is cross-referencing between the roadmaps.

9.2   Comparison of IEE to Total Quality Management

Often people suggest that Six Sigma is the same as total quality management (TQM). I do not agree. However, before making any generalities about the advantages of Six Sigma, it should be emphasized that there have been implementation and success/failure differences for both TQM and Six Sigma.

In my opinion, TQM did not systematically address the following itemized list with as much detail as Six Sigma. Six Sigma addresses most of the points in this list; however, IEE addresses all these items so that the concepts in Six Sigma/Lean Six Sigma are taken to the next level.

Some inherent advantages of using an IEE implementation are:

- Focus is given to bottom line benefits for organizations, where project monetary benefits are verified by finance. At the executive level, this breeds excitement since improvement work is being aligned to their primary measure of success.
- A support infrastructure is created where specific roles exist for people to be full-time practitioners (black belts) and other support/leadership roles (champions, green belts, and others).
- Practitioners follow a consistent project execution roadmap as describe in this book.
- Rather than a quality program, it is a business strategy that helps drive the business to the right activities correctly.

This point needs to be communicated and understood at the deployment onset.

- Projects are pulled for creation by the metrics that drive the business. However, often companies push for project creation, which may not be the best utilization of resources.
- Voice of the customer focus is given at both the satellite-level business metrics and 30,000-foot-level project execution metrics.

When implementing IEE, we need to capitalize on the lessons learned from other Six Sigma implementations. The Six Sigma benchmark study summary shown in Section A.2 of *Implementing Six Sigma* (Breyfogle, 2003) summarizes what six benchmarked companies have done.

My experiences for the success of IEE are consistent with the summary of common case study Six Sigma deployment attributes from Snee and Hoerl (2003):

Very Successful Case Studies	**Less Successful Case Studies**
• *Committed leadership*	• *Supportive leadership*
– Use of top talent	– Use of whoever was available
• *Supporting infrastructure*	• *No supporting infrastructure*
– Formal project selection process	– No formal project selection process
– Formal project review process	– No formal project review process
– Dedicated resources	– Part time resources
– Financial system integration	– Not integrated financial system

9.3   Initiating Deployment

Often organizations that are considering a Lean Six Sigma, Six Sigma, or IEE deployment make the statement that before deploying the system they want to conduct a pilot improvement project. With this approach, someone is trained and then applies the methodologies to improve a specified process. The success of the improvement project on making a business financial impact would then be the deciding factor whether to pursue a deployment.

On the surface, this approach sounds reasonable. However, a pilot project can fail for numerous reasons. One reason is that nondedicated people were to complete the project but no work time was allotted for the project or there was no, or too little, instructor-trainee project-application coaching. Another reason is that the process owner had no sense of urgency for project completion; the project's success had no impact on the performance measures of the process owner. One final cause for failure is that the pilot-trained person was someone who was available but did not have the characteristics for being an effective black belt.

Even if the pilot project was a great success, consider what it proved. The described tools in this book work. The only question is: How can the organization best get started and create an infrastructure to support it? The success of one project does not make for a successful deployment.

It has been said many times that traditional Six Sigma and Lean Six Sigma deployments need to be initiated at the executive level; a CEO project-driven deployment. Jack Welch used this approach when he initiated Six Sigma at GE. If the right people are selected to fill the roles, and a good Six Sigma infrastructure is created, there can be successful projects. However, even in the best deployment kick-offs and infrastructure, where the executive is committed, organizations have difficulty in sustaining a project search-and-completion deployment.

Traditional Six Sigma and Lean Six Sigma deployments create an organization in itself to search for projects and then complete them. Traditionally, the measure of success is the financial benefits from these projects. Reward systems for individuals can even be created that encourage the hunt for and completion of projects, which can often have little benefit for the system as a whole and drive the wrong activities. Often, even in the best find-our-next-project deployments, when the person who is leading the deployment leaves the company or has a position reassignment, the deployment loses much of its effectiveness.

As a business system that draws upon the many aspects of Six Sigma and Lean Six Sigma, IEE does not have the above deployment issues. When building the IEE system, it is best to start by building the enterprise process measurement and improvement system before project selection. The best way to build this infrastructure is by starting small and growing into a bigger system where the goal is to make the concepts of IEE and tools of Six Sigma and Lean a part of how work is done and not an add-on; not something extra that needs to be done.

A start-small-and-grow-big IEE deployment provides flexibility in that implementation can originate at a lower point in the management organization chart and then later grow throughout the business. This is analogous to the spreading of a warm-weather grass that is prevalent in the southern United States. Bermuda grass can be plugged since it grows in an outward direction through runners. Similarly, high-level executives need only be willing to introduce an IEE pilot-build in one portion of the business. Success of this business measurement and improvement system can then propagate throughout the business, similar to a Bermuda plug.

The purpose of the multi-volume series, *Integrated Enterprise Excellence: Beyond Lean Six Sigma and the Balanced Scorecard* (Breyfogle, 2008a, b, c) is to provide a consistent IEE message that fulfills various needs and desires. It will help bridge the gap between those who will execute the details, as described in Volume 3, and those who need a higher understanding level of the concepts, as presented in Volumes 1 and 2. With the proposed start-small-and-grow-big approach, executives can abort an implementation system at any time. For executives, this overall system has minimal downside risk and huge upside potential.

This approach is very different from the previously described pilot project approach. An IEE deployment can create a business system from which system performance measures pull for creating the best projects.

The foundation and system created during this deployment can springboard an organization into:

- Enterprise-wide alignment, metrics, tracking, and reporting standards
- Focus not only on how, but what, to measure
- Leaders are able to reduce firefighting by having the right measurements with the correct interpretations so that organizational efficiency and effectiveness improve

IEE deployment opportunities include:

- A business is new or relatively new to Lean Six Sigma
- A business has recently hired a deployment leader such as a master black belt to create a Lean Six Sigma infrastructure
- A Six Sigma or Lean Six Sigma deployment has been stalled

The basic steps for an IEE deployment are:

1. One or more black belts or master black belts work the IEE deployment as their certification project

2. The E-DMAIC structure is roughed out during a week-long, on-site workout near the end of their training
   a. Monday: Executive overview and kickoff
   b. Tuesday-Thursday: Provider facilitates with the trainee(s) and their team the building of an E-DMAIC structure tailored to their business
   c. Friday: Tailored E-DMAIC structure presentation to executive team
3. Trainee(s) moves the E-DMAIC structure to a working system, with provider's coaching
4. Build a network of resources to support the execution of the E-DMAIC business measurements and improvements

More information about an IEE deployment can be found at www.SmarterSolutions.com. Appendix A.1 includes a deployment provider selection matrix.

> A week-long IEE workout creates a first-pass system for the entire organization's E-DMAIC structure. At the end of the week, executives are presented the system, which includes, among other things, the organization's value chain with its performance measurements and reporting structure.

9.4 Stimulating Organizational Change

Consider that you like the IEE system that is described in this book; however, you don't know how to stimulate change.

Perhaps your company has a legacy system that people constantly work around. A cost of doing nothing differently (CODND) calculation for this system might provide the stimulus for change. Or, perhaps giving a book to the leading thinker, influencer or decision maker will help them understand the benefits of IEE. A copy of this book, or an appropriate volume from the three-book series described in the Appendix, would be excellent sources.

Appendix

Taking Lean Six Sigma and the balanced scorecard to the next level is described in *Integrated Enterprise Excellence: Going Beyond Lean Six Sigma and the Balanced Scorecard* (*Breyfogle 2008 a, b, c*). The three volumes in this series provide a roadmap for implementing Integrated Enterprise Excellence (IEE), which helps organizations overcome difficulties and shortcomings encountered with previous systems.

Volumes in this series provide the means to address the following frequently encountered problems:

- Business goals are not being met.
- Scorecards often lead to the wrong activities.
- Day-to-day firefighting of problems that don't seem to go away.
- Business strategies that are generic and/or difficult to translate to organizational work environments.
- Lean events and other improvement projects consume a lot of resources but often do not have much, if any, quantifiable benefit to the business as a whole.
- Lean Six Sigma:
    - Existing deployment projects which are either not completed on time, or reporting large financial claims that often cannot be translated into true benefits for the business as a whole.
    - Existing deployment that has stalled out and needs rejuvenation.
    - New deployment desires to create a system where improvement and design projects are in true alignment to business needs, and where projects are executed using an effective roadmap that truly integrates Six Sigma with Lean tools.

This series of three volumes describes how to orchestrate activities that can provide the highest yields at points where these efforts will have the greatest bottom line impact. In addition, focus is given in this orchestration so that activities will occur at the most opportune times throughout the entire organization.

Simply put, the described system helps an organization move toward the three Rs of business: everyone doing the Right things and doing them Right at the Right time throughout the organization. Rather than seeking out product or service flaws, this system determines whether the process itself is flawed. Rather than force projects where benefits could be questionable, designs and improvements are made that impact the overall systems for doing business. This system elevates every business unit to a new, more productive business way of life.

The ultimate goal for an enterprise management system is to achieve maximum, measurable, predictable, and sustainable bottom line results for the entire corporation. The volumes in this series describe an IEE business management system, which presents the structure and tools you can use to accomplish these objectives. This IEE methodology provides a power-enhancing performance measurement scorecard/dashboard system that serves as an enterprise-wide route to increase corporate profitability continually.

This series describes how IEE takes Lean Six Sigma and the balanced scorecard to the next level. This system helps organizations overcome some difficulties encountered with previous systems. In IEE, a value chain performance measurement system provides organizations with a no-nonsense metric system that leads to the orchestration of day-to-day value-added activities so that there is true business needs alignment. Improvement or design projects are created whenever business or operational metrics need betterment. This is in contrast to the search, selection, and creation of Six Sigma or Lean projects that often are not in true alignment with business goals. Organizations can gain a competitive advantage when this system becomes a business way of life.

Businesses that have adopted the Lean Six Sigma methodology have a built-in foundation for implementing this enhanced system. Others will learn how to establish a foundation for this system. For both groups, this series describes an enterprise process roadmap and a project execution roadmap, together with all the tools needed for enterprise excellence.

Volumes in this series describe the IEE system, which addresses the following example needs:

- Executives want a structured system that can assist them with meeting their financial goals.
- An organizational executive or a change manager is looking for an enterprise management structure that will coordinate, track, enhance, control, and help predict corporate results.
- Leadership wants to become more of a data-driven/data-decision-based company so that the right questions are asked before decisions are made.
- Executives want a system that helps them create a strategy that is more specifically targeted so that everyone has consistent focus toward meeting the organizational goals they would like to achieve.
- Company leadership wants to reduce the amount of waste that they routinely experience when fighting the problems of the day, which never seem to go away.
- Management wants a no-nonsense measurement and improvement system.
- Leadership wants a streamlined enhancement to their Sarbanes-Oxley (SOX) system so that the company benefits more from its implementation with less effort.
- Lean Six Sigma deployment leaders want to integrate Lean and Six Sigma concepts and tools so that they are using the right tool at the right time.
- Management wants to improve their performance measurement and improvement systems.
- Managers and practitioners want an easy-to-follow roadmap that addresses not only project execution but also enterprise issues.
- Organization leaders want a system that can help them orchestrate activities so that everyone is doing the right things and doing them right at the right time.
- Lean Six Sigma deployment leaders want a system that consistently leads to projects that are most beneficial to the overall enterprise.

CEO benefits from this series include:

- CEOs want to avoid the problem: "Chiefs (CEOs) are being pushed out of the door as directors abandon their laissez-faire

Table A.1: Where to start?

Where to start?		
Role	*I want to:*	*Source*
Executives, Champions, Managers, MBBs, BBs, GBs, and YBs	Assess the benefits of an IEE measurement and improvement system over other systems (novel format).	Volume 1
Executives, Champions, Managers, and MBBs	Understand the benefits of IEE when compared to other business systems and utilize a roadmap for IEE implemention at the enterprise level.	Volume 2
MBBs, BBs, GBs, and other practitioners	Execute effective process improvement projects, benefit from the project execution roadmap, and effectively utilize tools at both the project and enterprise level.	Volume 3

See Glossary for descriptions.

MBB = Master black belt   BB = Black belt   GB = Green belt   YB = Yellow belt

E-DMAIC (Roadmap): An IEE enterprise define-measure-analyze-improve-control roadmap, which contains among other things a value chain measurement and analysis system where metric improvement needs can pull for project creation.

P-DMAIC (Roadmap): An IEE project define-measure-analyze-improve-control roadmap for improvement project execution, which contains a true integration of Six Sigma and Lean tools.

approach to governance following the prosecutions at Enron Corp., WorldCom Inc., and other companies" (Kelly, 2006).
- CEOs want to create a legacy system of organizational efficiency and effectiveness, which outlives their tenure as company heads.
- CEOs want to create more customers and cash.

Table A.1 describes how the volumes of this series can address differing readers' needs and interests. Note that the syntax for figure or table references in this volume series is that the first number is the chapter number. The letter "A" was used in lieu of a number since the table is in the appendix.

SERIES DESCRIPTION: AN INTEGRATED SET OF REFERENCES

This book, *The Integrated Enterprise Excellence System: An Enhanced, Unified Approach to Balanced Scorecards, Strategic Planning, and Business Improvement,* introduced new perspectives on what to measure and report; when and how to report it; how to interpret the results; and how to use the results to establish goals, prioritize work efforts and continuously enhance organizational focus and success.

In the three-volume series, *Integrated Enterprise Excellence: Going Beyond Lean Six Sigma and the Balanced Scorecard* (Breyfogle 2008 a, b, c), there is both further elaboration on the shortcomings of traditional systems and the details of an IEE implementation. When explaining the concepts to others, readers can reference volumes or portions of volumes at the other person's level of understanding or need. Series volumes make reference to other volumes or *Implementing Six Sigma* (Breyfogle 2003) for an expansion of topic(s) or a differing perspective.

A content summary of this volume series is:

- *Integrated Enterprise Excellence Volume I – The Basics: Golfing Buddies Go Beyond Lean Six Sigma and the Balanced Scorecard* – An IEE onset story about four friends who share their experiences while playing golf. They see how they can improve their games in both business and golf using this system that goes beyond Lean Six Sigma and the balanced scorecard. The story compares IEE to other improvement systems.
- *Integrated Enterprise Excellence Volume II – Business Deployment: A Leaders' Guide for Going Beyond Lean Six Sigma and the Balanced Scorecard* – Discusses problems encountered with traditional scorecard, business management, and enterprise improvement systems. Describes how IEE helps organizations overcome these issues utilizing an enterprise process define–measure–analyze–improve–control (E-DMAIC) system. Systematically walks through the execution of this system.
- *Integrated Enterprise Excellence Volume III – Improvement Project Execution: A Management and Black Belt Guide for Going Beyond Lean Six Sigma and the Balanced Scorecard* – Describes IEE benefits and its measurement techniques. Provides a detailed step-by-step project define–measure–analyze–improve–control (P-DMAIC) roadmap, which has a true integration of Six Sigma and Lean tools.

Volumes of this series build upon each other so that readers develop an appreciation and understanding of IEE and the benefits of its implementation. Each volume and this book are also written to stand alone. Because of this, several concepts and examples are described in more than one book or volume. I also felt it was important to repeat key concepts in multiple publications because each book or volume is more than a discussion of tools and examples – that is, each book and volume presents IEE so that the reader gains insight into the interconnection of the concepts and how they can benefit from the techniques.

List of Acronyms and Symbols

Note: Some symbols used locally in the book are not shown.

ANOM	Analysis of means
ANOVA	Analysis of variance
BB	Black belt
BPIE	Business process improvement event
C&E	Cause-and-Effect (diagram)
CODND	Cost of doing nothing differently
COPQ	Cost of poor quality
CTQ	Critical to quality
DFIEE	Design for Integrated Enterprise Excellence
DFLSS	Design for Lean Six Sigma
DFSS	Design for Six Sigma
DMADV	Define–measure–analyze–design–verify
DMAIC	Define–measure–analyze–improve–control
DOE	Design of experiments DMAIC
DPMO	Defects per million opportunities
DPU	Defects per unit
EBIDA	Earnings before interest, depreciation, and amortization
ECMM	Enterprise cascading measurement methodology
E-DMAIC	Enterprise process DMAIC (roadmap)
EIP	Enterprise improvement plan
EPM	Enterprise process management
FG	Finished goods
GB	Green belt
IEE	Integrated Enterprise (process) Excellence
I-MR chart	Individuals control chart and moving range (same as *XmR* chart)

IPO	Input process output
KCA	Knowledge centered activity
KPIV	Key process input variable
KPOV	Key process output variable
LCL	Lower control limit
LDL	Lower decision level (in ANOM)
MBB	Master black belt
PDCA	Plan do check act
P-DMAIC	Project DMAIC (roadmap)
ROCE	Return on capital employed
RSM	Response surface methodology
S^4	Smarter Six Sigma Solutions
SIPOC	Supplier–input–process–output–customer
SPC	Statistical process control
Std. dev.	Standard deviation
TOC	Theory of constraints
TQM	Total quality management
TRIZ	Teoriya Resheniya Izobretatelskikh Zadatch (theory of problem solving)
UCL	Upper control limit
WIP	Work in progress or Work in process
XmR (chart)	SPC chart of individual and moving range measurements
	Mean of a variable x
YB	Yellow belt
μ (Mu)	Population true mean
σ (Sigma)	Population standard deviation

Glossary

Analysis of means (ANOM): An approach to statistically compare the means of individual groups to the grand mean.

Autocorrelation: In time series analyses, the correlation between values and previous values of the same series.

Balanced scorecard (the): The balanced scorecard (Kaplan and Norton, 1992) tracks business organizational functions in the areas of financial, customer, and internal business process, and learning and growth. In this system, an organization's vision and strategy lead to the cascading of objectives, measures, targets, and initiatives throughout the organization. This book describes issues with this system and an alternative IEE system that overcomes these shortcomings.

Baseline: Beginning information from which a response change is assessed.

Black belts (BBs): Six Sigma and IEE practitioners who typically receive four weeks of training over four months. It is most desirable that black belts are dedicated resources; however, many organizations utilize part-time resources. During training, black belt trainees lead the execution of a project that has in class report-outs and critiques. Between training sessions black belt trainees should receive project coaching, which is very important for their success. They are expected to deliver high-quality report-outs to peers, champions, and executives. Upon course completion, black belts are expected to continue delivering financial beneficial projects; for example, 4–6 projects per year with financial benefits of $500,000–1,000,000. Black belts can mentor green belts.

Black box: Describes a system where the interior operations are not known.

BPIE: *See* Business process improvement event system.

Burning platform: A term used to describe a sense of urgency; for example, the organization had a burning platform to improve their on-time delivery or they would loose their major customer's business.

Business process improvement event (BPIE) system: A system for identifying and timely resolving reoccurring problems. The resolution for these issues could lead to a simple agree-to procedure change, a DMADV design project, or P-DMAIC process improvement project.

Capability/performance metric: *See* Process capability/performance metric.

Cause-and-effect diagram (C&E diagram): This technique, sometimes called an Ishikawa diagram or fishbone diagram, is useful in problem solving using brainstorming sessions. With this technique, possible causes from such sources as materials, equipment, methods, and personnel are typically identified as a starting point to begin the discussion.

Champions: Executive level managers who are responsible for managing and guiding the Lean Six Sigma or IEE deployment and its projects.

Collins's three circles:

1. What can you do to be the best in the world?
2. What drives your economic engine?
3. What are you deeply passionate about? (Collins, 2001)

Common cause: Natural or random variation that is inherent in a process over time, affecting every outcome of the process. If a process is in control, it has only common cause variation and can be said to be predictable. When a process experiences common cause variability but does not meet customer needs it can be said that the process is not capable. Process or input variable change is needed to improve this situation; that is, this metric is creating a pull for project creation.

Continuous data (Variables data): Data that can assume a range of numerical responses on a continuous scale, as opposed to data that can assume only discrete levels.

Control: The term *in control* or predictable is used in process control charting to describe when the process indicates that there are no special causes. *Out of control* indicates that there is a special cause or the process is unpredictable.

Control chart: A procedure used to track a process with time for the purpose of determining if common or special causes exist.

Corrective action: Process of resolving problems.

Cost of doing nothing differently (CODND): COPQ within Six Sigma includes not doing what is right the first time, which can encompass issues such as scrap, reworks, and meetings with no purpose. To keep IEE from appearing as a quality initiative, I prefer to reference this metric as the cost of doing nothing differently (CODND), which has even broader costing implications than COPQ. In this book, I make reference to the CODND.

Cost of poor quality (COPQ): Traditionally, cost of quality issues have been given the broad categories of internal failure costs, external failure costs, appraisal costs, and prevention costs. See Glossary description for cost of doing nothing differently.

Customer: Someone for whom work or a service is performed. The end user of a product is a customer of the employees within a company that manufactures the product. There are also internal customers in a company. When an employee does work or performs a service for someone else in the company, the person who receives this work is a customer of this employee.

Dashboard: See Scorecard.

Days Sales Outstanding (DSO): In general, the average number of days it takes to collect revenue after a sale has been made. In the example in the text, it is the average number of days before or after the due date that a payment is received.

Defect: A nonconformity or departure of a quality characteristic from its intended level or state.

Defective: A nonconforming item that contains at least one defect or having a combination of several imperfections, causing the unit not to satisfy intended requirements.

Deming, Dr. W. Edwards: As an American statistician, Dr. Deming is known for his top management teachings in Japan after World War II. Dr. Deming made a significant contribution to Japan becoming renown for its high-quality, innovative products.

Design for Integrated Enterprise Excellence (DFIEE): A process used when developing new products, services, processes, or information technology (IT) projects. This development is efficient and effective with a focus on up-front understanding of customer requirements. IEE uses a DMADV process for DFIEE execution.

Design of experiments (DOE): Experiment methodology according to which factor levels are assessed in a fractional factorial experiment or full factorial experiment structure.

Discrete data (Attribute data): The presence or absence of some characteristic in each device under test; for example, proportion nonconforming in a pass/fail test.

DMAIC: Define–measure–analyze–improve–control Six Sigma roadmap.

DMADV: Define–measure–analyze–design–verify DFIEE/DFSS roadmap.

Dot plot: A plot of symbols that represent individual observations from a batch of data. Breyfogle (2008c) describes the creation of this plot.

DPMO: When using the nonconformance rate calculation of defects per million opportunities (DPMO), one first needs to describe what the opportunities for defects are in the process; for example, the number of components and solder joints when manufacturing printed circuit boards. Next, the number of defects is periodically divided by the number of opportunities to determine the DMPO rate.

Drill-down: A transition from general category information to more specific details by moving through a hierarchy.

E-DMAIC (Roadmap): An IEE enterprise define–measure–analyze–improve–control roadmap, which contains among other things a value chain measurement and analysis system where metric improvement needs can pull for project creation.

Enron effect: At the beginning of the 21st century, the executive management style in Enron and others companies lead to the downfall of these companies and executives spent time behind bars. In Enron, executive management had to do whatever it took to meet their numbers. Enron lacked metrics that gave a true picture of what was happening. This resulted in a smoke and mirror system which had integrity issues relative to the handling of business challenges. In addition, this system encouraged executive management to have no respect for either the financial or general well being of others, inside or outside the company. The catastrophic result of this management style is the Enron effect.

Enterprise cascading measurement methodology (ECMM): A system where meaningful measurements are statistically tracked over time at various functional levels of the business. This leads to a cascading and alignment of important metrics throughout the organization.

Enterprise improvement plan (EIP): A project drill-down strategy that follows: goal–strategies–high-potential area–projects.

Enterprise process management (EPM): Rather than having governance model that addresses initiatives as separate entities, in IEE a value chain EPM function can be created that orchestrates this system. The EPM function is responsible for integrating, overseeing, and improving the execution of these processes utilizing an E-DMAIC roadmap.

EPM: *See* Enterprise process management.

50-foot-level: A low-level view of a key process input variable metric; for example, process temperature when manufacturing plastic parts. This type of chart can involve frequent sampling, since special cause issues need timely identification so that problems can be quickly resolved without jeopardizing the quality or timeliness of the outgoing product or service.

Firefighting: The practice of giving focus to fixing the problems of the day or week. The usual corrective actions taken in firefighting, such as tweaking a stable process, do not create any long-term fixes and may actually cause process degradation.

Gantt chart: A bar chart that shows activities as blocks over time. A block's beginning and end correspond to the beginning and end date of the activity.

Governance, corporate: The system by which business corporations are directed and controlled. The corporate governance structure specifies the distribution of rights and responsibilities among different participants in the corporation, such as the board, managers, shareholders and other stakeholders, and spells out the rules and procedures for making decisions on corporate affairs. By doing this, it also provides the structure through which the company objectives are set, and the means of attaining those objectives and monitoring performance. Organization for Economic Cooperation and Development (OECD), April 1999.

Governance Model: The result from the people, committees, departments, and all others who make up a body for the purpose of administering something.

Green belts (GBs): Part-time Six Sigma or IEE practitioners who typically receive two weeks of training over two months. Their primary focus is on projects that are in their functional area. The inference that someone becomes a green belt before a black belt should not be made. Business and personal needs and requirements should influence the decision whether someone becomes a black belt or green belt. If someone's job requires a more in-depth skill set, such as the use of design of experiments, that person should be trained as a black belt. Also, at deployment initiation, black belt training should be conducted first, so that this additional skill set can be used when coaching others.

Hidden factory: Reworks within an organization that have no value and are often not considered within the metrics of a factory.

Histogram: A graphical representation of the sample frequency distribution that describes the occurrence of grouped items.

Hoshin kanri: Japanese name for policy deployment. Used by some Lean companies to guide their operational strategy.

Hypothesis: A tentative statement, which has a possible explanation to some event or phenomenon. Hypotheses are not a theoretical statement. Instead, hypotheses are to have a testable statement, which might include a prediction.

IEE: *See* Integrated Enterprise Excellence.

IEE scorecard/dashboard metric reporting process:

1. Assess process predictability.
2. When the process is considered predictable, formulate a prediction statement for the latest region of stability. The usual reporting format for this statement is as follows:
   a. When there is a specification requirement: nonconformance percentage or defects per million opportunities (DPMO).

b. When there are no specification requirements: median response and 80 percent frequency of occurrence rate.

IEE Workout: See Workout (IEE).

In control: The description of a process where variation is consistent over time; that is, only common causes exist. The process is predictable.

Individuals control chart: A control chart of individual values where variability between subgroups affects the calculated upper and lower control limits; that is, the width between the upper and lower control limits increases when there is more variability between subgroups. When plotted individuals chart data is within the upper and lower control limits and there are no patterns, the process is said to be stable and typically referenced as an in control process. In IEE, this common cause state is referenced as a predictable process. Control limits are independent of specification limits or targets. Breyfogle (2008c) describes the creation of this chart.

Information technology: Computer systems and applications, which involves development, installation, and/or implementation.

Infrequent sub-grouping/sampling: Traditionally, rational subgrouping issues involve the selection of samples that yield relatively homogeneous conditions within the subgroup for a small region of time or space, perhaps five in a row. For an $\bar{x}$ and R chart, the within-subgroup variation defines the limits of the control chart on how much variation should exist between the subgroups. For a given situation, differing subgrouping methodologies can dramatically affect the measured variation within subgroups, which in turn affects the width of the control limits. For the high-level metrics of IEE, we want infrequent subgrouping/sampling, so that short-term variations caused by KPIV perturbations are viewed as common cause issues; that is, typical process variability is to occur between subgroups. This type of control chart can reduce the amount of firefighting in an organization. However, this does not mean that a problem does not exist within the process. Volume 3 describes some approaches to view the capability/performance of our process, or how well the process meets customer specifications or overall business needs. When process capability/performance improvements are needed for these metrics, we can initiate an IEE project; that is, IEE projects are pulled into the system, as they are needed by the metrics. Examples of infrequent subgrouping/sampling are:

1. ROI was tracked monthly over the last three years on an individuals control chart.
2. One paid invoice was randomly selected daily and the difference between payment receipt date and due date was tracked for the last year using an individuals control chart, where the data had a lognormal transformation).
3. The mean and standard deviation (log of standard deviation was plotted) for all DSO invoices collected were tracked for the last year using individuals control charts, where approximately the same number of invoices was received and tracked weekly.
4. Daily, the number of defects was divided by the opportunities and plotted on an individuals control chart with an appropriate transformation, where approximately the same number of opportunities occurred daily.

Integrated Enterprise (process) Excellence (IEE, I double E): Integrated Enterprise Excellence (IEE) is a sustainable business management governance system, which integrates business scorecards, strategies, and process improvement, so that organizations move toward the three Rs of Business. (Everyone is doing the Right things and doing them Right at the Right time.) IEE provides the framework for innovation and continual improvement, which goes beyond Lean Six Sigma's project-based defect and waste reduction methods. The existence and excellence of a business depends on more customers and cash; that is, $E = MC^2$. As a business way of life, IEE provides the organizational orchestration to achieve more customer and cash. The IEE implementation roadmap provides direction on the creation of an enterprise process system in which organizations can significantly improve both customer satisfaction and their bottom line. The techniques help manufacturing, development, and service organizations become more competitive and/or move them to new heights. IEE is a structured approach that guides organizations through the tracking and attainment of organizational goals. IEE integrates enterprise process measures and improvement methodologies with tools such as Lean and theory of constraints (TOC) in a never-ending pursuit of excellence. IEE becomes an enabling framework, which integrates, improves, and aligns with other initiatives, such as total quality management (TQM), ISO 9000, Malcolm Baldrige Assessments, and the Shingo Prize.

Inventory turns: The number of times that a company's inventory cycles or turns over per year.

ISO 9000: The International Organization for Standardization (ISO) series of developed and published standards. The intent of these standards is to define, establish, and maintain an effective quality assurance system in both manufacturing and service industries.

IT: *See* Information technology.

Jim Collins's three circles: See Collins's three circles.

Kaizen Event or Blitz: An intense short-term project that gives focus to improve a process. Substantial resources are committed during this event; for example, Operators, Engineering, Maintenance, and others are available for immediate action. A facilitator directs the event, which usually includes training followed by analysis, design, and area rearrangement.

Law of physics: A physical law, or a law of nature, that is considered true.

Lean: Improving operations and the supply chain with an emphasis on the reduction of wasteful activities like waiting, transportation, material hand-offs, inventory, and overproduction.

Level Five System: Jim Collins (2001) describes in *Good to Great* a level five leader as someone who is not only great when they are leading an organization but who enables the organization to remain great after they leave it. I describe the level-five-leader-created legacy as being a *Level Five System*.

Malcolm Baldrige Award: An award that recognizes yearly up to five companies that demonstrate outstanding quality management systems. The award, started in 1986, would later be known as the Malcolm Baldrige National Quality Improvement Act which was created under the direction of ASQ and the National Institute of Standards and Technology. The Act established a national award that recognizes total quality management in American industry.

Master black belts (MBBs): Black belts who have undertaken two weeks of advanced training and have a proven track record delivering results through various projects and project teams.

They should be a dedicated resource to the deployment. Before they train, master black belts need to be certified in the material that they are to deliver. Their responsibilities include coaching black belts, monitoring team progress, and assisting teams when needed.

Mean: The mean of a sample $\bar{X}$ is the sum of all the responses divided by the sample size. The mean of a population (μ) is the sum of all responses of the population divided by the population size. In a random sample of a population, $\bar{X}$ is an estimate of the μ of the population.

Median: For a sample, the number that is in the middle when all observations are ranked in magnitude. For a population, the value at which the cumulative distribution function is 0.5.

Metric: A measurement that quantifies a particular characteristic.

Mini Kaizen: Recognizes that the best expert for a job is the person who does the job. Everyone is encouraged to make small improvements that are within their power to implement. The collection of thousands of small improvements can have a major impact. Its implementation requires both conscious and subconscious day-to-day and minute-by-minute thinking about improvements by all employees. Required also is that these employees possess this type of thinking skills.

Nonconformance: Failure to meet specification requirement.

Out of Control: Control charts exhibit special causes conditions. The process is not predictable.

Pareto chart: A graphical technique used to quantify problems so that effort can be expended in fixing the "vital few" causes, as opposed to the "trivial many." Named after Vilfredo Pareto, an Italian economist.

Pareto principle: 80 percent of the trouble comes from 20 percent of the problems, that is, the vital few problems.

PDCA: *See* Plan do check act.

P-DMAIC (Roadmap): An IEE project define–measure–analyze–improve–control roadmap for improvement project execution, which contains a true integration of Six Sigma and Lean tools.

Plan do check act (PDCA): Frequently referred to as the Deming cycle or Shewhart cycle. Sometimes the check step is replaced with a study step; that is, PDSA. PDCA has the following components: Plan–Recognize a need for change that establish objectives and process for delivering desired results; Do–Implement change that is to be assessed; Check–study results and identify lessons learned; Act–Use lessons learned to take appropriate action. If change was not satisfactory repeat the process.

Population: Statistically a population is a group of data from a single distribution. In a practical sense, a population could also be considered to be a segment or a group of data from a single source or category. In the process of explaining tools and techniques, multiple populations may be discussed as originating from different sources, locations, or machines.

Predictable process: A stable, controlled process where variation in outputs is only caused by natural or random variation in the inputs or in the process itself.

Preventive action: An action that is taken to eliminate from re-occurrence a potential nonconformity cause or other undesirable situation.

Probability plot: Data are plotted on a selected probability paper coordinate system to determine if a particular distribution is appropriate (i.e., the data plot as a straight line) and to make statements about percentiles of the population. The plot can be used to make prediction statements about stable processes. Breyfogle (2008c) describes the creation of this plot.

Process capability/performance metric: IEE uses the term process capability/performance metric to describe a process's predictive output in terms that everyone can understand. The process to determine this metric is:

1. An infrequent subgrouping and sampling plan is determined, so that the typical variability from process input factors occurs between subgroups, for example, subgroup by day, week, or month.
2. The process is analyzed for predictability using control charts.
3. For the region of predictability, the noncompliant proportion or parts per million (ppm) is estimated and reported. If there are no specifications, the estimated median response and 80 percent frequency of occurrence is reported.

Process flow diagram (chart): Path of steps of work used to produce or do something.

Pull: A Lean term that results in an activity when a customer or downstream process step requests the activity. A homebuilder that builds houses only when an agreement is reached on the sale of the house is using a pull system. *See* push.

Pull for project creation: This term is derived from the Lean term, pull. An IEE deployment objective is that performance metric ownership is assigned through the business value chain, where metric tracking is at the 30,000-foot-level. In the E-DMAIC process, the enterprise is analyzed as a whole to determine what performance metrics need improvement and by how much so that whole organizational goals can be met. These metric improvement needs would then create a pull for project creation. *See* push for project creation.

Push: A Lean term that results in an activity that a customer or downstream process step has not specifically requested. This activity can create excessive waste and/or inventory. A homebuilder that builds houses on the speculation of sale is using a push system. If the house does not sell promptly upon completion, the homebuilder has created excess inventory for his company, which can be very costly. *See* pull.

Push for project creation: This term is derived from the Lean term, push. Lean Six Sigma deployments create and execute projects that are meant to be beneficial to the business. However, when assessing the typical Lean Six Sigma project selection process, we note that either a deployment steering committee or some level of management selects projects from a list that they and others think are important. For this type of deployment, there is often a scurry to determine a project to work on during training. I refer to this system as a push for project creation; that is, people are hunting for projects because they need to get certified or meet a certain goal. With this deployment system, there can be initial successes since agree-to low hanging fruit projects can often be readily identified and provide significant benefits; however, it has been my experience that this system of project determination is not typically long lasting. After some period of time, people have a hard time defining and/or agreeing to what projects should be undertaken. In addition, this project creation system does not typically look at the system as a whole when defining projects to undertake. This system can lead to suboptimization, which could be detrimental enterprise as a whole. Finally, this Lean Six Sigma deployment system typically creates a separate function entity that manages the deployment, which is separate from operational scorecards and functional units. In time, people in these functions can be very visible on the corporate radar screen when downsizing forces occur or there is a change in executive management, even though the function has been claiming much past success. *See* pull for project creation.

Radar chart: A chart that is sometimes called a spider chart. The chart is a two-dimensional chart of three or more quantitative variables represented on axes originating from the same point.

Rolled throughput yield (RTY): For a process that has a series of steps, RTY is the product of yields for each step.

Root cause analysis: A study to determine the reason for a process nonconformance. Removal or correction of the root cause eliminates future nonconformance from this source.

Satellite-level: Used to describe a high level IEE business metric that has infrequent subgrouping/sampling so that short-term variations, which might be caused by the variation key input variables, will result in control charts that view these perturbations as common cause variations. This metric has no calendar boundaries and the latest region of stability can be used to provide a predictive statement of the future.

Scorecard: A scorecard is to help manage an organization's performance through the optimization and alignment of organizational units, business processes, and individuals. A scorecard can also provide goals and targets, which help individuals understand their organizational contributions. Scorecards span the operational, tactical, and strategic business aspects and decisions. A dashboard displays information so that an enterprise can be run effectively. A dashboard organizes and presents information in a format that is easy to read and interpret. In this series of book volumes, I refer to the IEE performance measurement as either a scorecard or scorecard/dashboard.

Shewhart control chart: Dr. Shewhart is credited with developing the standard control chart test based on 3σ limits to separate the steady component of variation from assignable causes.

Shingo prize: Established in 1988, the prize promotes awareness of Lean manufacturing concepts and recognizes United States, Canada, and Mexico companies that achieve world-class manufacturing status. The philosophy is that world-class business performance may be achieved through focused core manufacturing and business process improvements.

Sigma: The Greek letter (σ) that is often used to describe the standard deviation of data.

Sigma level or sigma quality level: A quality that is calculated by some to describe the capability of a process to meet specification. A six sigma quality level is said to have a 3.4 ppm rate. Pat Spagon from Motorola University prefers to distinguish between sigma as a measure of spread and sigma used in sigma quality level (Spagon, 1998).

SIPOC (supplier-input-process-output-customer): Is a tool that describes the events from trigger to delivery at the targeted process.

Six Sigma: A term coined by Motorola that emphasizes the improvement of processes for the purpose of reducing variability and making general improvements.

SMART goals: Not everyone uses the same letter descriptors for SMART. My preferred descriptors are italicized in the following list: S: *specific*, significant, stretching; M: *measurable*, meaningful, motivational; A: agreed upon, attainable, achievable, acceptable, action-oriented, *actionable*; R: realistic, *relevant*, reasonable, rewarding, results-oriented; T: *time-based*, timely, tangible, trackable.

Smarter Six Sigma Solutions (S⁴): The term used in this book to describe the *wise* and unique application of statistical techniques to creating meaningful measurements and effective improvements.

Smarter Six Sigma Solutions assessment (S⁴ assessment): A term introduced in the first edition *Implementing Six Sigma* (Breyfogle, 2003). The methodology uses statistically based concepts while determining the *best* question to answer from the point of view of the customer. Assessment is made to determine if the right measurements and the right actions are being conducted. This includes noting that there are usually better questions to ask to protect the customer than "What sample do I need?" or "What one thing should I do next to fix this problem?" IEE resolution may involve putting together what are traditionally considered as separate statistical techniques in a smart fashion to address various problems.

Special cause: Variation in a process from a cause that is not an inherent part of that process. That is, it's not a common cause.

Stakeholders: Those people or organizations who are not directly involved with project work but are affected its success or can influence its results. They may be process owners, managers affected by the project, and people who work in the studied process. Stakeholders also include internal departments, which support the process, finance, suppliers, and customers.

Standard deviation (σ, s): A mathematical quantity that describes the variability of a response. It equals the square root of variance. The standard deviation of a sample *(s)* is used to estimate the standard deviation of a population (σ).

Statistical process control (SPC): The application of statistical techniques in the control of processes. SPC is often considered to be a subset of SQC, where the emphasis in SPC is on the tools associated with the process but not on product acceptance techniques.

Statistical quality control (SQC): The application of statistical techniques in the control of quality. SQC includes the use of regression analysis, tests of significance, acceptance sampling, control charts, distributions, and so on.

Stock options: A stock option is a specific type of option with a stock as the underlying instrument; that is, the security that the value of the option is based on. A contract to buy is known as a call contract, while a contract to sell is known as a put contract.

Stories: An explanation for the up-and-down from previous quarter or yearly scorecard/dashboard metrics. This is not dissimilar to a nightly stock market report of the previous day's activity, where the television or radio reporter gives a specific reason for even small market movements. This form of reporting provides little, if any, value when it comes to making business decisions for a data-driven company.

Sub-grouping: Traditionally, rational sub-grouping issues involve the selection of samples that yield relatively homogeneous conditions within the subgroup for a small region of time or space, perhaps five in a row. Hence, the within-subgroup variation defines the limits of the control chart on how much variation should exist between the subgroups. For a given situation, differing sub-grouping methodologies can dramatically affect the measured variation within subgroups, which in turn affects the width of the control limits. For the high-level metrics of IEE, we want infrequent subgrouping/sampling, so that short-term KPIV perturbations are viewed as common cause issues. A 30,000-foot-level individuals control chart, which is created with infrequent sub-grouping/sampling, can reduce the amount of firefighting in an organization. However, this does not mean that a problem does not exist within the process. IEE describes approaches to view the process capability/performance, or how well the process meets customer specifications or overall business needs. When improvements are needed to a process capability/performance metric, we can create an IEE project that focuses on this need. IEE projects have a pull for project creation system when metric improvements are needed.

The balanced scorecard: See balanced scorecard (the).

Theory of constraints (TOC): Constraints can be broadly classified as being internal resource, market, or policy. The outputs of a system are a function of the whole system, not just individual processes. System performance is a function of how well constraints are identified and managed. When we view a system as a whole, we realize that the output is a function of the weakest link. The weakest link of the system is the constraint. If care is not exercised, we can be focusing on a subsystem that, even though improved, does not impact the overall system output. We need to focus on the orchestration of efforts so that we optimize the overall system, not individual pieces. Unfortunately, organization charts lead to workflow by function, which can result in competing forces within the organization. With TOC, systems are viewed as a whole and work activities are directed so that the whole system performance measures are improved.

30,000-foot-level: A Six Sigma KPOV, CTQ, or Y variable response that is used in IEE to describe a high-level project or operation metric that has infrequent subgrouping/sampling so that short-term variations, which might be caused by KPIVs, will result in charts that view these perturbations as common-cause issues. It is not the intent of the 30,000-foot-level control chart to provide timely feedback for process intervention and correction, as traditional control charts do. Example 30,000-foot-level metrics are lead time, inventory, defective rates, and a critical part dimension. There can be a drill-down to a 20,000-foot-level metric if there is an alignment; for example, the largest product defect type. A 30,000-foot-level individuals control chart can reduce the amount of firefighting in an organization when used to report operational metrics. As a business metric, 30,000-foot-level reporting can lead to more efficient resource utilization and less playing games with the numbers.

Three Rs of business: Everyone doing the Right things and doing them Right at the Right time.

Throughput, TOC: The rate of generating money in an organization. This is a financial value-add metric which equates to revenues minus variable costs.

TOC: *See* Theory of constraints.

TOC throughput: *See* Throughput, TOC.

Total quality management (TQM): A management program, which works on continuous product or service improvements through workforce involvement.

TQM: *See* Total quality management.

Value chain: Describes flowchart fashion both primary and support organizational activities and their accompanying 30,000-foot-level or satellite-level metrics. An example of primary activity flow is: develop product – market product – sell product – produce product – invoice/collect payments – report satellite-level metrics. Example support activities include IT, finance, HR, labor relations, safety and environment, and legal.

Visual factory: Management by sight. Visual factory involves the collection and display of real-time information to the entire workforce at all times. Work cell bulletin boards and other easily-seen media might report information about orders, production schedules, quality, delivery performance, and financial health of business.

Voice of the customer (VOC): The identification and prioritization of true customer needs and requirements, which can be accomplished through focus groups, interviews, data analyses, and other methods.

Voice of the process (VOP): A quantification of what the process delivers. A voice of the process to voice of the customer needs assessment can identify process improvement focus areas; for example, a 30,000-foot-level assessment indicates an 11 percent delivery-time nonconformance rate.

WIP: A general description for inventory that is being processed within an operation or is awaiting another operation.

Work in process (WIP): *See* WIP.

Work in progress (WIP): *See* WIP.

Workout (IEE): An IEE workout is a week-long concentrated effort to build the E-DMAIC framework; that is, a kaizen event to create the E-DMAIC framework. Typically on Monday there is a one-day executive workshop, which among other things describes IEE and its structure. On Tuesday through Wednesday the facilitator works with an IEE in-house technical team and others to build the E-DMAIC framework with its process drilldowns. On Friday, a two-hour report out of the customization of the E-DMAIC system, as described on Monday, is presented to the executive team that attended the Monday session. This presentation will include, among other things, a comparison of a sample of their 30,000-foot-level metric report outs with their current reporting methods. After the week-long session, the workout facilitator will continue work with the IEE in-house technical team to continually refine their E-DMAIC system.

Yellow Belts (YBs): Process improvement team members who typically receive three days of training, helping their effectiveness in the participation of project executions, such as data collection, identifying voice of the customer, and team meetings.

References

Austin (2004), http://www.ci.austin.tx.us/budget/eperf/index.cfm.

Babich, P. (2005), *Hoshin Handbook*, third edition, Total Quality Engineering. Poway, CA.

Breyfogle, F. W. (1992b), *Statistical Methods for Testing, Development, and Manufacturing*, Wiley, Hoboken, NJ.

Breyfogle, F. W. (2003), *Implementing Six Sigma: Smarter Solutions® using Statistical Methods*, second edition, Wiley, Hoboken, NJ.

Breyfogle, F. W. (2008a), *Integrated Enterprise Excellence Volume I – The Basics: Golfing Buddies Go Beyond Lean Six Sigma and the Balanced Scorecard*, Bridgeway Books, Austin, TX.

Breyfogle, F. W. (2008b), *Integrated Enterprise Excellence Volume II – Business Deployment: A Leaders' Guide for Going Beyond Lean Six Sigma and the Balanced Scorecard*, Bridgeway Books, Austin, TX.

Breyfogle, F. W. (2008c), *Integrated Enterprise Excellence Volume III – Improvement Project Execution: A Management and Black Belt Guide for Going Beyond Lean Six Sigma and the Balanced Scorecard*, Bridgeway Books, Austin, TX.

Breyfogle, F. W. (2008d), *The Integrated Enterprise Excellence System: An Enhanced, Unified Approach to Balanced Scorecards, Strategic Planning and Business Improvement*, Bridgeway Books, Austin, TX.

BusinessWeek (2007), Six Sigma: So Yesterday?: In an innovation economy, it's no longer a cure-all, McGraw Hill, June 11. New York, NY.

Collins, J. (2001), *Good to Great: Why Some Companies Make the Leap... and Others Don't,* HarperCollins Publishers Inc., New York.

Cunningham, J. E. and Fiume, O. J. (2003), *Real Numbers: Management Accounting in a Lean Organization,* Managing Times Press, Durham, NC.

Davenport, T. H. and Harris, J. G. (2007), *Competing on Analytics: The New Science of Winning,* Harvard Business School Publishing Corp., Boston, MA.

Deming, W. E. (1986), *Out of the Crisis,* Massachusetts Institute of Technology, Cambridge, MA.

Drucker, P. F. (1954), *The Practice of Management,* Peter F. Drucker.

Foxconn (2006), Foxconn Strategy, http://www.foxconn.com/about/strategy.asp.

Goldratt, E. M. (1992), *The Goal,* second edition, North River Press, New York.

Hambrick D. C. and Fredrickson J. W. (2001), *Are you sure you have a strategy?* Academy of Management Executive, Vol. 15(4). Briarcliff, Manor, NY.

Hamel, Gary and Prahalad, C. K. (1994), "Competing for the Future," *Harvard Business Review,* July–August.

Hindo, B. (2007), At 3M, A Struggle Between Efficiency And Creativity: How CEO George Buckley is managing the yin and yang of discipline and imagination, *BusinessWeek,* McGraw Hill, June 11. New York, NJ.

Jackson, T. L. (2006), *Hoshin Kanri for the Lean Enterprise,* Productivity Press, NY.

Kaplan, R. S. and Norton, D. P. (1992), "The Balanced Scorecard – Measures that Drive Performance," *Harvard Business Review,* Jan.–Feb.

Kelly, J. (2006), *CEO firings at a record pace so far this year: Leaders are getting pushed aside as boards, wary of Enron-type problems, become more vigilant,* Bloomberg News, Austin American Statesman, October 1.

Lloyd, M. E. (2005), *Krispy Kreme knew early of slowing sales, suit says*, Austin American Statesman, Business Briefing, Dow Jones Newswire, January 4.

Petruno, Tom (2006), *Options Inquiries Smell of Scandal*, Austin American Statesman, Business & Personal Finance, Los Angeles Times Article, July 16, 2006.

Richtel, Matt (2007), *Dell, Admitting Managers Inflated Sales Reports, Will Restate Income*, New York Times, August 17, 2007.

Snee, R. D. and Hoerl, R. W. *Leading Six Sigma: A Step-by-Step Guide Based on Experience with GE and other Six Sigma Companies*, Prentice Hall, 2003.

Spagon, P. (1998), personal communications.

Spear, S. J. and Bowen, H. K. (1999), Decoding the DNA of the Toyota Production System, *Harvard Business Review*, September. Boston, MS{AQ2}.

Thurm, S. (2007) "Now, It's Business By Data, but Numbers Still Can't Tell Future," *Wall Street Journal*, July 23, page B1.

US Dept of Interior (2003), *OMB and Bureau Scorecard Actions: Getting to Green*, http://www.doi.gov/ppp/scorecard.html.

Womack, J. P. and Jones, D.T. (1996), *Lean Thinking*, Simon & Schuster. New York, NY.

Index